PERSON AND PSYCHE

The Institute for the Psychological Sciences Monograph Series

GENERAL EDITOR: *Craig Steven Titus*

The Institute for the Psychological Sciences (IPS) Monograph Series publishes original scholarly works that promote studies in the broad field of the psychological sciences. The Institute espouses the view that interdisciplinary conversations among experts in psychology, philosophy, and religion serve to advance our understanding of what constitutes both the mental well-being and the spiritual flourishing of the human person.

The overall mission of IPS is to contribute to the renewal of the Christian intellectual tradition and to the development of a psychology consistent with the teachings of the Catholic Church. IPS remains committed at the same time to fruitful dialogue with voices from outside the Christian tradition. The Institute offers M.S. and Psy.D. degrees in clinical psychology and an M.S. degree in general psychology. Moreover, it initiates research projects through the Scholarly Research Center located in Arlington, Virginia, and the Centre for Philosophical Psychology established since 2004 at Oxford.

The IPS Monograph Series is placed under the patronage of St. Albert the Great, a thirteenth-century man of science and faith, whose life incarnates the human values that the Institute for the Psychological Sciences aims to promote. Those scholars associated with IPS seek to maintain a constructive and critical conversation based on both advanced research about and a high vision of the human person. IPS is committed to integrating what is the best in faith-based traditions and what is judged worthwhile in the several life sciences.

*The Institute for the Psychological Sciences
Monograph Series*

VOLUME 2

PERSON AND PSYCHE

Kenneth L. Schmitz

The Institute for the Psychological Sciences Press
Arlington, Virginia

Distributed by:
The Catholic University of America Press
620 Michigan Ave., N.E. / 240 Leahy Hall
Washington, DC 20064

The paper used in this publication meets the minimum requirements
of American National Standards for Information Science—Permanence of Paper for Printed Library Materials, ANSI Z39.48-1984.
∞

LIBRARY OF CONGRESS CATALOGING-IN-PUBLICATION DATA
Schmitz, Kenneth L.
    Person and psyche / Kenneth L. Schmitz.
        p. cm. — (The Institute for the Psychological Sciences mono-
graph series ; v. 2)
        Includes bibliographical references (p.   ) and index.
        ISBN 978-0-9773103-7-1 (pbk. : alk. paper)   1. Ontology.
2. Metaphysics.   3. Psychotherapy.   4. Psychology and
philosophy.   I. Title.
        BD331.S393 2009
        128—dc22   2008055295

CONTENTS

ACKNOWLEDGMENTS

I would like to express my gratitude to the innumerable persons who have taught me—teachers, students, and others—and especially to Dr. Gladys Sweeney, Academic Dean of the Institute for the Psychological Sciences, who made me more conscious of the relation between our two disciplines, however faulty my understanding may yet be; to Dr. David McGonagle, Director of the Catholic University of America Press, whose knowledgeable encouragement gave me confidence to reach somewhat beyond my own discipline; and to Dr. Jude Dougherty, Dean Emeritus of the School of Philosophy at the Catholic University of America, whose friendship, reaching back half a century, has so often opened up for me new avenues of thoughtful research.

This book was researched and in large part written while I was in residence at the Institute for the Psychological Sciences' Centre for Philosophical Psychology in Oxford. At that time, I benefited from the support of the Dominicans at Blackfriars Hall, University of Oxford; Father Richard Finn, O.P. (the Blackfriars' Head of Hall and Regent of Studies), was especially helpful in facilitating fruitful contacts. Moreover, I enjoyed the generous hospitality of the Brothers of the Christian Schools while in Oxford.

The following pages have benefited from the constructive input of those professors and students who attended my seminars given at Blackfriars Hall (University of Oxford) and at the Institute for the Psychological Sciences (Arlington, Virginia).

Finally, I would like to express thanks to Susan Barnes for her careful copyediting that went beyond managing commas to help clarify my reflections. I would also like to thank Gregory Bottaro for helping with the indexes and Craig Steven Titus for guiding the book through its various stages.

INTRODUCTION

Psychology and philosophy are distinct studies, each within its own domain; yet they are close neighbors. By its nature philosophy invites us to the comprehensive and intensive study of the very being of things—to the study of their existence, their basic and original character—and also to reflection upon the fundamental interrelationship of things to each other, with especial attention to the human 'thing': to ourselves and each other within the overall relation of all things to each other. But while philosophy reaches out to the very concrete status of things and their basic structure as well as their community with all other things, the form its language takes must needs be general, expressing the nature of each and every being while affirming its unique status. Psychology reaches out to certain things in a more special way, tracing out the specific nature of the human psyche in as precise a way as it can. Indeed, it is just this approach that provides so much detailed understanding of the inner workings of what tradition has called the soul, and which encompasses conscious feelings, images, and ideas, as it reaches down even into the depths of the subconscious.

It is clear that the aims of the two studies differ, yet in an intimate way they search out the same object—or rather, subject—the human person. Whereas philosophy in its anthropological form studies the union and unitary interplay of soul and body, of mind and matter, psychology—in its distinctive way—concentrates on consciousness. The difference in the two approaches may be initially expressed in terms of context; for while philosophy considers the whole human person—mind and body—it does so in the larger context of the values of being, situating its analysis and reflection within the horizon of being as such, and in its most penetrating depth within the absolutely original principle of existential actuality, that actuating energy that sustains each and every being. Psychology, on the other hand, takes as its context, not the whole horizon of being, but the specific totality of human consciousness. For that reason alone, its scope is more restricted, but its study of the structures of human consciousness is more detailed. It seeks out a descriptive understanding of the acts of consciousness—of emotion, imagination, ideation, and willed action, as well as the subliminal border of explicit attention. In its positive dimension, psychology directs its reflections to the healthy functions of consciousness, applying its findings to the maintenance of a healthy personality. In psychotherapy it also seeks out the malfunctions of consciousness—of obsession, addiction, depression, and the like, with a view to reestablishing a healthy human life.

What is remarkable about the difference in the two approaches, philosophical and psychological, is the intimate relation—for all their difference—that exists between a truthful understanding of both aspects of what is, after all, a single consciousness in each singular human person. There is no sense of an indiscriminate fusion of these two distinct approaches; rather, there is an intimate interplay, in which philosophy can provide a foundation and horizon for the life of consciousness as that same life engages in the very activities so precisely analyzed by psychology. Indeed, psychic health is just this participation of these two dimensions within the integrity of the human person.

In the following chapters—since I am a philosopher—I reflect upon the general foundation of all and every being, with especial reference to human beings (Chapter 1). This is followed by reflection upon the dynamics with which we are endowed in the very origins

of our human nature (Chapter 2). In the third chapter, these two pri-
or principles are taken up into the sphere of human freedom with the
value and promise that it holds for the human person. While advert-
ing in the earlier chapters to some aspects of psychological research, it
is in the concluding chapter that I take up some of the issues that arise
in psychology and psychotherapy. I aim to search out their significance in terms of the transcendental characteristics of being—with
especial attention to truth, goodness and beauty—and in terms of the
primitive inclinations with which our human nature is endowed, and
thereby to take these up into that freedom that is our crown and exal-
tation, even as it penetrates and transforms the human psyche.

My own limited understanding of the contributions of psychological thought has been refreshed and deepened by the paradoxical
character of ourselves as persons. For the human person is at once
both unique in its presence, and yet relational with others; most interior of all beings, yet most open to others, not only to other humans
but to all being. These properties of relational uniqueness and open
interiority are the channels through which the transcendental "traf-
fic" of being and the more determinate pre-occupations of our human nature engage the texture of being as these same properties situate us within the universe of reality and in the companionship with
other beings. For our relational consciousness engages others—family, society, and other regions of being—as we search for knowledge
and shape our actions, hopefully and at our best, open to truth and
the perfective power of being, but also conscious of admiration at the
panoply of being, and open in its most exalted form, even to adora-
tion.

PERSON AND PSYCHE

one

⁀

THE CONVERGENCE OF *PERSONA* AND *PSYCHE*

The Ontology of the Person

I propose to set out upon a journey of reflection, a journey on which we will attempt to traverse the distance between philosophy and psychology—more particularly, between metaphysics and psychotherapy. What makes this journey possible is the shared context within which the distance is traversed, for both disciplines in their distinct ways are concerned with the human person. And although a philosophical interest in the person is, first of all, theoretical, it has practical consequences; whereas psychotherapy, while it is ordered to practical outcomes, whether in remedial cure or in the positive advancement of personal health, is grounded in an understanding of the subject of its practice, i.e., in theoretical presuppositions about the person, attested to in empirical and narrative *experiment.*

As in any adventure, it is best that it have a goal and some sense of the steps towards that goal. If the goal is an enriched understanding of the human person, insofar as the joint efforts of philosophy and psychology can contribute, the steps—of the present modest and tentative philosophical effort—recommend themselves as follows by way of a four-part development of the theme: We begin with a *metaphysical* interpretation of the person, pass from that to the specific dynamics of *anthropology,* from that to the distinctive presence of the personal, to conclude with the concrete contribution of *psychotherapy.* It is an ambitious journey, promising a fuller and deeper collaborative understanding of the human person than either discipline, on its own, provides.

Let us begin, then, with what philosophy has to say about the human person. The scope of philosophy, understood metaphysically, as the philosophy of being, is meant to embrace the full range of all that exists, along with the potentialities that are resident in actual beings. Moreover, a traditional form of metaphysics rests this all-embracing vision in the ultimate ground of a First and Continuing Cause that is Itself the purity of Being-as-such. It would seem to follow from such a breadth, such a grandness of vision, however, that the distinctness of the person is in danger of being lost. Indeed, an understanding of being seems farthest removed from the specificity and even the particularity of the human person. What, after all, does the seemingly abstract notion *being* have to contribute to an understanding of the person?

To answer that question, we must ask what we mean by the term 'being.' No doubt, it is the most universal of all terms, embracing everything that exists. But it is not an ordinary universal genus, able to embrace all that is simply because it is empty of content. Indeed, it was just this empty misconception of being that allowed Hegel to get his famous dialectic underway, since such an understanding of being is equivalent to nothing *(das Nichts).* From that identification-indifference the movement of opposites could begin, leading to the Absolute System in Hegel, and by an inversion of theory and practice, to the dialectic of Revolution in Marx. In these understandings, being has been confined within the polarities of rational thought, between the universal and the particular, so that an all-important factor has been assumed but not articulated, and so overlooked.

But suppose that we take another look at this comprehensive term 'being,' and recognize in it the *actuality of presence*. This introduces a quite different polarity and energy than that of the general and the particular so familiar to the natural and social sciences. The ordinary sense of the term, from which philosophy must build its technical meaning, includes the actuality of presence, as when, with Hamlet, we say: "to be or not to be." Now, the factor of presence within the meaning of the term 'being' indicates that the term is no ordinary abstract universal, no ordinary genus, caught up in the dynamic between an empty universality and a fragmentary particularity, but rather that which transcends the division of abstract and concrete, of empty and full, of the partial and the complete, of the universal and particular, since it includes these states within itself. Indeed, being is best expressed by the term 'omnipresence,' which joins both universality and particularity with actuality, since it expresses both the comprehensive and the intensive character of being, its all-enhancing and its all-penetrating character. If there is a dialectic at work in such an understanding of being, it is not that of the universal and the particular, but that of being and non-being, of presence and absence. For in penetrating to the depth of what is, we arrive at this dramatic division between being and nothing that is so fundamental as to be neither an opposition, nor even a difference, but rather thought's own way of acknowledging the wonder of presence.

And yet, the very wonder of presence does lead to an experience of absence, as when we remember an absent friend or a long-past event, for in a strange way absence does "exist" as absence-in-the-presence of either memory or expectation, and even in the subhuman world as included in the results of past events, as past growth is registered in the rings of trees.

And so we are led to a fundamental distinction between what I will call 'being' and what I will call 'reality'. By this distinction I mean that, while being is co-extensive with presence as intimately including it within its very meaning, reality includes *negativity* of several kinds. The very limitation of the beings we encounter in our daily rounds and in ourselves is signed by that negativity; none are the fullness of being as such. There is, however, a further distinction to be made, a distinction between simple negations (as when a limited, finite being is not all that there is), and a *privation,* by which we mean a lack within a being that is not part of what the being is meant to be (as when we suffer memory loss, or sickness, and ultimately, death). Nor is the subhuman realm devoid of the privations and the defects that make up reality as we encounter it.

Now, the import of the distinction between being and reality is that it allows us to highlight the *actuality* that is characteristic of being. And it invites us to explore further the character of being that is present within reality, and to explore the texture of being that is resident within the mixture that is reality. In so doing we venture into a somewhat paradoxical realm, to wit: for limited terms, such as 'dog' and 'cat', or 'mineral' and 'vegetal', we can say that the one is not the other, but for the term 'being' we cannot accept such restrictions, because it reaches out beyond the farthest stars to include everything in the universe, and yet reaches down into the very depths of each thing, into its very interiority. Being, though, does not stop even at the division between the exterior and the interior, between what is beyond and what is within. And for that reason, it reaches into the remarkably intimate actuality of each human person, and even into the most ordinary thing, if we can even use such a minimal term as 'ordinary' when speaking of any and every thing.

Now, as we explore the character of being, we bear in mind that, no matter how absolutely general the name we give to the properties of being, they too designate what is most universal and yet most particular, most abstract yet most concrete; they provide the most fundamental and all-inclusive insight into what each of us is as members of the universe of being; and they provide the most original and basic indication of our constitution as persons, for we too are beings.

To enter into the *ontological* constitution of the person, I propose that we revisit a capital text in which Thomas Aquinas sets forth what he terms the 'transcendental properties' of being. The transcendental properties are those characteristics that, while as close to being as color is to its surface, and constituting its very identity, they thereby consequently attend being wherever it is found, whether in the outreaches of the starry skies or within the very vitals of each person, entering into the very texture of the person in the most basic and intimate, the most original and originative, way.

In highlighting the person as the *focus* of both a philosophical as well as a therapeutic concern—and before I take up the closer examination of the transcendental properties of being—let me remark upon another mode of reflection that is shared by philosophy and psychotherapy. Like all disciplines, both find their context within what I consider the four *basic modes* of discourse. These fundamental ways of thinking and speaking of reality have been exercised throughout the more than two millennia of so-called Western culture, a culture whose birthplace is largely in Greece and Judaea, with later contributions from Rome, Islam, and Europe.

Modern disciplines are, for the most part, mixes of these four basic paths of discourse. All of these find their origin in classical Greece. They seem to have originated in the Greek discovery of grammar. By that term, I do not mean excellence in the use of one's language, since in every culture we find poets, story-tellers, and rhetoricians of grace and brilliance. Grammar, however, is the intellectual study of the linguistic elements by which we give an account of our experience, whether of realities or dreams. It is not the study of all of the uses of language, but an *analytic* study of the components of language, primarily in its theoretical use as giving an account of the way things are and are experienced.

Grammar seems to have originated around the eighth century B.C. as the Greeks shaped their language in a literary fashion from the hieroglyphs of the Phoenician language. This was to transfer the written form of language from a primarily (and highly reduced) visual and pictorial form to a literate sign-system, which relied more upon the ear than upon the eye, incorporating vowels and consonants in the alphabet, so-called from the first two letters of the Greek written language (alpha-beta). Now, this literacy seems to have freed the Greek mind for a more abstract re-entry into the world of meaning, and into the world of which they were speaking and writing. This move to auditory abstraction seems to have set up the means for the liberation of thought, which then expressed itself in four fundamental ways of giving an account of things encountered.

The order of the appearance of these four modes is not clear, and the four seem to be closely associated with one another. The move from the study of grammar to its exfoliation into the branches of language study led to the subdisciplines of logic, rhetoric, analytics, and topics (to cite the Aristotelian categorization). The aim of grammar was to identify the various verbal forms and their function in expression, as well as the proper ordering of argument. This subset of studies concentrated upon the word *(logos)*. But number *(arithmos)* also claimed a role with the study of mathematics, especially among the Greeks, with the translation of Egyptian land measurement into *geometria*, the abstract study of quantified forms. The Greek genius concentrated especially upon this branch of the study of number, due to the Greek failure to develop a competent language for the articulation of mathematics, which was to await further development in India and Arabia.

So far, then, discourse was ordered to the articulation and expression of word and number. But history *(istoria)* developed also according to discourse measured by time and events. Finally, philosophy *(philosophia)* appeared, at least as early as Thales and the Ionian physicists and—with Parmenides—it gave expression to the study of being.

In sum, then, *word, number, time,* and *being* constitute the four basic modalities of methodical, reflective discourse; subsequent disciplines have appropriated them and combined them in diverse ways.

In this schema, philosophy is primarily ontological discourse about the principles of being, while as rational wisdom *(phronesis, sophia, sapientia)* it is open to the other modes as ordering them in a certain way. In its own way, psychotherapy also avails itself of all four: of language in psychoanalytic narrative, of time in memory retrieval, of number in statistical testing, and—at least in some forms—of the ontological in terms of basic conceptualization.

As we review the history of these modes of explanatory discourse, we might think of each as, at one time or another in the intellectual history of Western culture, making a claim to providing first philosophy, i.e., claiming to be the most fundamental mode of discourse and explanation, the most basic way of giving a rational account. As we review this history, we see that—for the most part, but by no means without challenge—*ontology,* or discourse about being, held sway throughout the ancient and mediaeval periods—indeed, up until the Renaissance, when *linguistics* took first place briefly. With the development of a modern scientific interest, however, in the seventeenth century, *mathematics,* in the form of astronomy and physics, and later with chemistry, took first place, so that even philosophy conformed to the modality of mathematics, as with Descartes' four rules of method.

None of these modes of discourse ever entirely disappeared or relinquished its claim to priority in rational reflection. Philosophy, while it toiled on in the mode of metaphysics and the study of being, in the early modern period for the most part lost its pride of place, supplanted by the succession of forms that claimed to be first philosophy. In the eighteenth century, however—and then in explosive fashion in the nineteenth—history took first place in contributing to our basic understanding of reality, so that not only in the realm of human agency and events but in the nonhuman cosmos itself, an account in terms of development and time held sway, especially in geology and evolutionary biology. And finally, more recently, in the twentieth century, linguistics, not in the literary form of the Renaissance but in the more logical form of language analysis, claimed the role and rank of first philosophy, while—in something of a countermovement—phenomenology took steps to restore being (especially with Heidegger, but also with Husserl) to its former rank. I, too, will make the attempt to restore ontology to its former place as the most suitable claimant to the place and role of first philosophy.

Permit me a brief personal reference for purposes of analogy. Many years ago, as a navigator in the Canadian Air Force I plotted the course of the airplane across the night skies by means of the constancy of the stars. I would leave my desk in the nose of the aircraft, make my way along the plane to its midsection, where I would place myself under a glass bubble, take out my sextant, and probe the sky for the brighter stars. As I took their measure, they served as a visible compass with which to guide us on our journey.

So, too, in our search for understanding, the transcendental properties of being serve as beacons of intelligible light that illuminate our path, shining in the mixture of light and dark, of being and nonbeing, that makes up the reality we encounter on our journey through life. For those properties, like the stars, are the beacons that illumine our way, guiding us by their intelligibility, their abiding trustworthiness and their luminosity. It was always best to take my measure from two or three stars, carrying the readings back to my desk where, translated into the appropriate numbers, they could be charted on my map, telling us where we were and where we were going. As I sighted those stars through my sextant, their light entered in some small way into my vision and my mind, to be converted into the measured numbers that were then transferred to my chart.

So, too, the transcendentals, not as numbers but as properties of beings—especially the three that go by the name of truth, goodness and beauty *(verum, bonum, et pulchrum)*—are infallible guides to our progress. For they are great luminaries in the texture of being, shining with the glory of that first creation, which, despite the storms of evil and privation that beset us, are like a great compass in the firmament of being, redolent with the power to guide us towards a fuller humanity.

Their power to guide us lies in the nature of things, which are not merely *factual states of affairs,* somehow to be acknowledged and then dealt with in accordance with our desires and power, but rich deposits of meaning and value that offer themselves to us. The positivists, such as August Comte and others, will tell us not to press our questions beyond the surface of the facts that confront us, since all that we have at our disposal is the *facticity* that arrests the mind and bends it back upon itself. We are told that the mind encounters an insurpassable barrier to further and deeper penetration. To the contrary, however, the way of reflection suggests that *factuality* hides within itself the *actuality* of being. As we move, then, from factuality to actuality, we are led more deeply into a consideration of the texture of being and its transcendental properties.

As we turn to consider the facts about being, we might begin with its energy, that *energeia* that Aristotle found at the center of being. Still caught up in the Greek love of form, he tended to treat that energy as exhibited primarily in the coming to be of substantial being. No doubt, the Christian experience has been a religious and theological stimulant to further deepening the understanding of that primal energy. Deeper reflection carried the mind past the formal features of the things it encountered—none of which were, in the last instance, able to account for their own existential presence—to a deeper, transformal core within them.

To be sure, in a kind of ancient mode of surface thinking, the question of ultimate and absolutely original presence could be ignored, as in anticipation of modern positivism. One could say that things were always there in a cosmos without origin, but that left one asking: *What* precisely was it that was always there, and *how* did it come to be there? Not being already there, but coming-to-be, coming-into-being, seized the mind. Then, as the mind took more seriously the question of the origin of the beings we encounter, it raised the existential question. To put it in the modern form that Leibniz gave it and Heidegger reworked: Why anything at all, why not rather nothing?

In addressing this question, St. Thomas radically deepened a distinction that he found in Avicenna. The latter, focusing upon the quiddities or forms of things, had distinguished their existence from their essence, and had—in the Latin version that was available to Thomas—differentiated those essences that possessed their own identity in themselves and those that also were joined to existing states. The primary direction of the mind was towards the formal identity of things. The Latin translation of Avicenna considered existence a mere condition that pertained to some essences. St. Thomas accepted the distinction between essence and existence, but he raised existence *(esse, actus essendi)* to the highest principle of actuality. In so doing, he joined the Latin *esse* to the Greek *energeia;* for *Thomas,* esse *is* that absolutely first principle in each and every thing that transcends and energizes its formal identity. This radically changes the relation of essence and existence, of the formal and the existential principles that constitute each and every being. For the original energy that activated each being in its formal identity as essence, not only made it to be *what* it is, but made it to be *simpliciter; esse* is thus seen as the first principle, which confers existential presence upon all the other factors in each and every being.

The notion of a principle of actuality that transcends the formal or structural principles in the make-up of things is not an easy principle for the mind that tends to seek rest in the formal identity of things, in what they are. And indeed, the transformal principle of *esse* can go awry, as when in the existentialism of John-Paul Sartre the mind rejects all receptive relation to essences, leaving its energy to be turned this way or that in accord with our choices. Nevertheless, if we stop to wonder at the very presence of things, including ourselves, who have received our being from elsewhere, we are led to acknowledge that the very complex that makes up the identity of each thing, including ourselves, is brought into existence and kept in existence through a principle of *actuating presence*. It is just this principle that entitles each thing to be called a being *(ens)*.

Of course, we never encounter simple existence, but always existing *things (res)*, with a determinate character. Each actuality possesses an identity that is its own and is distinguishable from other beings. This formal property consists of a core identity which is recognized as the stable center of the kind of being each thing is *(res)*, its *essential* character or substance, but the more expansive formal structure of the thing includes much more, some of it relatively stable, other characteristics more transitory, so that we can speak of the *essence* of the thing in the stricter sense (substance) and also in the broader looser sense (accidents).

Now it is the more stable core that places the being in a certain category that is the basis for the specific way it behaves. Every student of chemistry knows what to expect from the various elements and compounds and can formulate the laws of action and reaction, of combination and discombination. So, too, with organic beings, and finally with humans. We see, then, that the formal principle, the essential principle, lays the ground of what, for the human species, constitutes natural law and, for non-human species, scientific law.

So far then, we have the two principles of *esse* (actuality or power) and *essence* (subtantiality or structure). The union of these first two principles, of existence and essence, constitutes the third transcendental property: the ontological unity characteristic of each and every being *(unum)*. Now the ontological unity of a being differs from the formal unity of nature or essence, a unity that a being shares with others of the same kind, and the ontological unity of a being also differs from the unitary identity of each of the being's accidental characteristics. Whereas the thing's nature or essence identifies it as a member of a specific kind of being, the ontological unity consists precisely in the communion of existence and essence that constitutes it as an individual being, the union of existential energy and formal structure.

Beings, however, are not closed off from one another, but are part of that ordered set referred to as the cosmos. The relations into which each enters differs in accordance with the kind of being that it is, which in turn is determined by its stable substance as well as its transitory characteristics. Yet the fuller consideration of the being of each thing must also take into account its real and potential capacity for relations with other beings, i.e., fuller consideration must make reference to others (*aliquid,* otherness). Now, as we join the unity of each indvidual being with its relationality *(aliquid),* we arrive at the recognition of the community of beings. We find, therefore, that at its most expansive range of consideration, philosophy takes as its horizon the community of being *(communitas rerum).* It is in this encompassing notion that one situates both the radical diversity of each being and the community they share as participants in being. This is an integration of radical unity and diversity that transcends formal difference and identity in constituting the analogical community of beings.

With the recognition of the relationality inherent in the community of beings, we come upon three distinctive modes of that relationality. As the mind goes out to reach the reality of the beings it encounters, it finds them meaningful, though it may also become aware that it never exhausts the fullness of that meaningfulness. This constitutes the intelligibility or truth of beings *(verum),* their native solidarity and connatural friendship with an enquiring mind.

In speaking of the truth of beings, an important acknowledgment is being certified, namely, that, whereas the truth of the things we encounter may come to actual rest in our minds, it is not our minds but the truth of being that is the ground that, along with our capacity, makes possible this coming to rest. Indeed, the depth of their intelligibility is confirmed by the long history of intellectual enquiry that constitutes not only philosophy but the ongoing research of the sciences and ordinary common sense questioning as well. The greatest confirmation of the intelligibility of things is the bottomless depth of meaning that is shed from what can only be called a mystery of light.

But that light holds its attraction, too, and this is the ground for speaking of the goodness of things *(bonum).* This phrase does not mean that all things are indiscriminately good for all other things. It does mean that each being holds within itself the excellence endowed by existence and by the formal character that confers upon it its unity, relationality, and intelligibility. Not only the philosopher, but the psychotherapist as well, passes through the truth of the person in search of the good that will further his or her well-being, through cure or development.

Before we take up the last of the transcendental relations, beauty (*pulchrum*), it will be well to recall our earlier distinction between the texture of being and the mixture that constitutes reality. The transcendental properties heretofore described are, for the most part, mixed with negativity, as the therapist knows too well. The unity of a thing may suffer disintegration (character); the relationality of things may be destructive (conflict); the intelligibility of things be distorted and darkened (illusion); the desirability of things conflicted (negation); and so, too, with beauty and its luminosity. Just as disunity disrupts the unity of being, error its intelligibility, evil its goodness, so too the ugly may mar the face of being. Yet being never fails to resist and to survive in injured fashion, so that we can still discern the luminosity of being even in an ugly complex, and can search to find how its disorder can be repaired. That is the sign of the hope that is resident in the texture of being and that calls for the courage to discern the texture of being even in the darkest mixture of reality. It is this that the therapist searches for as helpmate in his endeavors.

⤸

As we return to the first transcendental property, the transformal and electric character of existence, we might consider three ways of addressing it in our thought. The first is the positivist way, which is to dismiss it arbitrarily as beyond the possibility of comprehension. But we do make sense of it, inasmuch as we recognize the absolute division between what exists and what does not. The question can be set aside only by admitting defeat and by giving absolute value to some other, less primary, factor, such as chance or necessity or evolution.

A second strategy would be to incorporate existence within the cosmos itself as embodying its own existence. The problem with such a strategy, however, is that the cosmos is an ordered set of finite, limited beings, each of which has received its existence from an other, while none of the others in the set justify their existence. It is something like magic, therefore, to confer upon the set a quality of such importance without finding in the set as such a source for such a transcendent quality.

It remains, then, to attribute the existence which all things receive in the ordered set to a cause of existence which does not itself receive existence but already possesses and communicates it. This is precisely the First Cause of Being that is addressed by the various proofs for the existence of a First Principle. I recognize that what has been said so far does not constitute a formal proof; it is enough that it ensures that the insight is not irrational, but sufficiently rational to await determination by demonstrative proof. Since this proof would take us far afield, it is enough for us to leave the hypothesis of a cause of existence as a reputable question and position, and to highlight the peculiar character of the issue of the origin of the beings we encounter.

Now, it is just this combination of origin and destiny, of beginning and end, that is found in the texture of being. The fundamental origin is to be found in the creative source of existence, the coming into being out of nothing. We might think this wholly outside our experience, but as a matter of fact it is not quite. Suppose that a favorite object of ours is burned—a book, the last letter from a dear friend, some memento of a deep and cherished friendship. The beloved object may be reduced to ashes. Are we to say: "Well, it has not disappeared. It has not ceased to exist"—because of the ashes that remain? To be sure, *something* remains, so that we cannot speak directly of existence and nonexistence; but the beloved object no longer exists, and the ashes are poor substitutes. We experience the loss of being *ad nihilum*, its reduction as such to nothing, since the ashes in no way fulfill the absence. Less obvious, but just as truly, we experience the arrival in being of something that has not been, such as a beloved child, or a beautiful work of art. One might say in the case of the child that the parents pre-existed the child, that something pre-existed the child; but the child did not. Or again, that the paint and canvas of a work of art pre-existed, so that what has occurred is a reformulation of the elements. That is true, but the painting *as an entity* did not pre-exist, at least not until it began to form in the artist's sensibility and imagination and to receive its own existence through his hands. And yet, if no creature is endowed with the power of bringing into existence, these examples of coming-to-be seem to be by participation in and cooperation with the cause of being.

To be sure, we are not creators *ex nihilo,* since we bring things into being out of pre-existing materials. It is not that *we* are creators *ex nihilo,* but that the things we encounter come into existence and pass out of existence in the community of beings. It is here that participation has a role to play, for we participate in the coming-into-being and the passing-out-of-being within a community of being that transcends us and is prior to us, both temporally and ontologically. Our action is initiated between the poles of creation and participation, both of them moving within the community of being in which we find ourselves as members. We must be very precise here: we are not creators *ex nihilo,* but we are participants in the coming-to-be and passing away of the *being* of others; we are secondary agents whose causality can—by participating in the causality of the Cause of existence—bring about the coming-into-being and the passing-out-of-being of things. But we can do this only by virtue of the general causality of the First Cause.

Once again, we must be precise here. We are not creators of existence absolutely, *ex nihilo,* but we do experience coming-into-being and passing-out-of-existence as we engage with the beings we encounter. This is enough to provide us with an intuition of radical absence, and to illumine our joy in a new being and its presence—enough to provide us with wonder at such original and originating presence and absence. We are not creators *ex nihilo* as though, unassisted, we bring beings into existence in a radical way, but our causality does participate in and reflect at a secondary level the horizon of presence and absence in the household of being. The reliance of secondary causes upon the Cause of Being does not compromise that First Cause, since it has conferred upon the texture of being and upon the community of beings their own integrity. But as participants in the rhythms of existence we play a subordinate role in the presence and absence of things. It is just this attunement with the logic of being that plays itself out in our thought and in our actions. And it is just this ontological dynamic that we possess as persons and participate in through our search for the intelligibility and truth of things, and seek out through our love of the good of things, and admire in wonder at the beauty of things. It is through participation in the luminous properties of being that we resonate with the very ontological make-up of ourselves and the ontological constitution of the community of being of which we are personal members. And is this not the basis of psychotherapy? By way of analogy, we might speak of ourselves as participants in the symphony of being, not its conductor. We are at once both instruments and recipients of its most striking transcendental properties, for our discovery of truth confirms the ontological logic of the community of beings, just as our admiration and wonder at its luminosity confirms the transcendental character of its beauty.[1] The transcendental properties of being that reside within the human person as our fundamental constitution and yet reach out beyond the furthest reaches of our knowledge provide both a compass for our thought and action and also a testament to the glory of that creation of which we are singular members.

1. Cf. Joseph Ratzinger (now Pope Benedict), in his *'In the Beginning . . .': A Catholic Understanding of the Story of Creation and the Fall,* trans. Boniface Ramsey, O.P. (Grand Rapids, MI: Wm. Eerdmans, 1995), speaks of "God's logic," "the logic of the universe," and the "rhythm of God's love" (pp. 26–27), and of beauty as the "radiance of the truth of things" (p. 30).

two

⤳

THE INCLINATIONS OF NATURE

The Anthropology of the Person

As we move within, to the specific character of the human person—
that which both sets the person off from other beings and yet also
relates the person to others in distinctively human ways—we do not
leave the transcendental properties of being behind; rather, we find
them playing a role in the very constitution of the specificity of what
it means to be human. Those very transcendental properties that enter into the constitution of the person as a being now take on more
specific roles in the process of human development and typology[1] in
defining what it means to be a human person.

1. A. Damasio, *The Feeling of What Happens: Body, Emotion and the Making of Consciousness* (London: Vintage, 2000), pp. 143–44, remarks upon "the organism's invari-
ance and the impermanence of permanence," adding: "although the building blocks for
the construction of our organisms are regularly replaced, the *architectural designs* [ital-
ics mine] for the varied structures of our organisms are carefully maintained. There is

As the transcendental property of ontological unity *(unum)* comes into play, the unity of each being is realized as an essential unity *(essentia, res)*. Precisely, as ontological, the unity of existence and essence *(esse/essentia)* is what composes every individual being; but, in considering the composite unity of the human being, we now turn our attention to the specific unity of the essence or nature of our composite being. This consideration no longer attends explicitly to the unity of essence and existence, but to the specific character of the essence in the line of formal causality. The existential presence is assumed but not explicitly adverted to. We now leave metaphysics for the philosophy of nature, and precisely for the philosophy of human nature, i.e., for philosophical anthropology and the typology of the human person.

The term 'nature' today is popularly identified with what is not human, with forests and sea, with plants and animals, but traditionally it has been understood as a principle present and operative within human beings as the basic formative factor, as when we speak of 'human nature'. Now, the study of human nature is bordered on two sides: by the philosophy of being on the one side and by the positive sciences on the other. On the one hand, it is distinct from the metaphysical recognition of the deeper, transformal principle of existence *(actus essendi),* which is the first principle in the ontological order of analysis.[2] It is too easy to dismiss the role of human nature in favor of the existential interest in the human person, as in the philosophy of existentialism. On the other side, however, the philosophical consideration of human nature can also be dissolved into the particularity of the positive sciences, which look past the unity of the essential

---

a *Bauplan* for life [italics his] and our bodies are a *Bauhaus* [italics his]." And further: "No component remains the same for very long. . . . What remains the same, in good part, is the construction plan for our organism structure and the set points for the operation of its parts. Call it the spirit of the form and the spirit of the function" (p. 144). This "design" is precisely what traditional philosophers refer to as the substantial form, and which more popularly in the human is called the soul.

2. Indeed, Thomists have distinguished between metaphysics, which studies the being of things, and the philosophy of nature, which concerns the formal principle without adversion to the principle of *esse*.

nature we possess as members of the human race in favor of the complexity of the organization that constitutes our specific identity.

From both sides, then—from the comprehensive horizon of metaphysics, and from the detailed study of scientific elements and organization—the very concept of human nature is all but lost sight of. Some metaphysicians suppress the philosophy of nature as somehow to be taken for granted but not given over to serious study—thus tending to surrender it exclusively to positive science; positive scientists too often explore the wonderful interaction of the various elements that make up the human complex, seeing in that interaction not the unity of a being with a distinctive nature but the complex organization of a system. The scientist in pursuit of his own calling to detail the analysis of the parts, and the metaphysician caught up in the transformal study of existence, may both fail to explore the specificity of that *unum* that is not only the unity of a being, nor only the unity of an organization or organism, but the mediating unity of the specific nature by which membership in the community of beings is secured for us as humans—since the principle of human nature mediates between the ontological unity of our being and the systemic organization of our material parts.

Among the transcendental properties of being, including that of ontological unity (*esse*/essence = *ens* or entity) and within the formal identity of the nature (*essentia* or *res*), there is also the principle of finality *(bonum)*. For the nature of each being is born for what we might term a further career. Even the simplest chemical element and the most basic atomic particle is destined for interaction, for combination and discombination, and with others, for integration in broader relationships and larger contexts. In the more complex units of being, the very term 'nature', deriving from the term *nascitur*, being born, is—so to speak—born for further development.[3] So too with human nature—it is destined to growth towards maturity in the individual. So

3. Modern theories of evolution propose a description of the unfolding of natural varieties, but—by the very character of their enterprise—they cannot investigate the question of radical origin and so do not provide an explanation.

that, along with the existential principle *(esse)* and the principle of formal identity (essence), we have the principle of development as growth towards a pre-given end (telos). We have here, then, three constitutive principles—existential, formal, and final causality—playing out their roles on a material base (material causality) in the constitution and realization of our human nature, all together realizing the stages of the development of the human individual in his or her being.[4]

While such a manifold concept of our human nature, embodying not only the formal aspect but the final as well, is alien to many thinkers today, nevertheless it is surreptitiously assumed as operative in their expectation of a relatively constant behavior and tendency, which is taken for granted in the confidence with which they approach familiar things.[5] We expect chemicals to combine or repel, fire to burn, seeds to grow—barring no obstacle—birds to fly, fish to swim, and carnivores to eat more than lettuce. These truths seem hardly worthy of mention, yet their suppression or dismissal removes a formal mediating principle of order from the cosmos and its interwoven set of natured things. Nature as the principle of behavior and development is inherent in each of the things we encounter. The question in many sophisticated minds is whether such an obvious principle of common-sense order is worthy of further reflection and of being taken up as an important principle of interpretation and explanation.

It is curious how easily the concept of the stability of the natures

---

4. The three-fold role of the principles of nature (existential, formal, and final causality) embodies the three-fold modality of time, in which the concrete and expanded "now" contains not only the temporal moment of the present but also the immediate past (retention) and the immediate future (protention), as Husserl has shown in his analysis of time-consciousness.

5. For example, John Bowlby is emphatic in rejecting teleology as lying outside his own methodology, which uses instrumental terms, such as "goal-directed" and "feedback," in order to remain within his positivist methodological presuppositions. He replaces the concept of causality with that of function. See especially chapter 8 of *Attachment*, vol. I of his trilogy *Attachment and Loss* (New York: Basic Books/Perseus Group, 1969, 1982). See Works Cited in the present volume for vols. II and III of that trilogy.

of things, their more or less permanent typology, is overlooked in learned discourse as a real principle of identity and action; at best, it is used to catalogue various natural kinds in terms of phyla, genera, and species. At most then, the specific principle of nature has retreated to serve modestly only in taxonomy without any deeper significance. Beyond doubt there are in reality combinations whereby things of one nature are joined with another to form a hybrid, such as a fruit that partakes of both the apple and the pear; and there is the domestic enhancement of the qualities of plants and animals through cross-varietal breeding. But these results rely upon the relatively stable identity of distinct natures in things.

Nevertheless, the modern style of thought does not attend closely to the permanence of nature, in part because of the prominence of an anti-traditional exaggeration of the concept of progress and novelty. In the matter of origins we have August Comte advising against such enquiry into origins on the grounds that it can lead nowhere, and that enquiry ought to be restricted to the description of behavior formulated into laws, preferably quantitative ones. In a more expanded sense, Marx is so bold in his defense of future-oriented revolutionary practice that he insists that social and political advance can be intellectually secured only if we interpret all past activity as due to human agency; having made ourselves the agents of all past activity—and thus allegedly having been the sole authors of the past—we now have the absolute right to alter the present in favor of our vision of the future.

There is no denying, also, the astounding advances in technology, which have vastly increased human control over the environment, control reaching even into matters affecting our health. This has had positive effects in the cure of diseases but dubious effects through technological intervention in the reproductive processes, as well as massive pollution of atmosphere, land, and sea. Already in the early stages of modernity, Francis Bacon had advised us to learn to imitate nature in its processes, but so that we might control nature by directing it exclusively to the satisfaction of our aims and desires. Even earlier (and perhaps nowhere more strikingly), the freedom of man from nature was declared in the Renaissance treatise by Pico della Mirandola entitled *The Fable of Man,* in which we read that God had given to each created thing its own nature. When He came to the creation of man, He found that He had no natures left to give, and so He gave man freedom instead: freedom without nature, without the stability and pre-given directives of our human nature.

An analogous advocacy of a natureless freedom was taken up in the past century by the existentialist Jean-Paul Sartre, who so elevated free choice that it—and it alone—confers value on external things insofar as they serve the individual's denatured freedom. Even Descartes so preferred his rational method—lodged in and devised to meet the demands of the enquiring ego—that he advises us to intervene in the analysis of ideas in the interests of the clarity and distinctness required by the human mind in its project of filtering the objective order through its own rules of method (see Rules II and III of the *Discourse on Method*). Moreover, that method was to serve the practical human interest and project of mechanical control and medicinal practice.[6] And later, in the reputed defense of human reason, Kant filtered the evidence of his senses through the subjective grid of space and time, and organized the resultant phenomena in accordance with the categories of the understanding, so that the mind could reach only that which conformed to its a priori constitution, resulting in the reduced knowledge of things as they appear not as they are, i.e., as they appear within the structure of the human subject and not as they are in themselves and in nature.

A more balanced and articulate understanding of nature in premodern times acknowledged our access to the relative stability of natured things, along with their particular and individual variety. Today we rightly acknowledge the passing away of past life forms and the emergence of new ones. But this acknowledgment does not deny or

6. He also intended to formulate an ethics in accordance with the rules of his method, though he never completed the task.

obscure the transcendental condition that the beings we encounter come into being with relatively stable essential forms or natures. Indeed, we encounter the principle of stable formal unity in ourselves as the mark of our own human nature, and it is to that principle that we now attend, for without it we have no ground for our common humanity and for the rights and duties that attend it. As with every nature—but in a very distinctive way with human nature—the principle of nature unfolds in three phases: the originative, the normative and the consummative; that is, as originating, as guiding and as completing our humanity, thus embracing the effective cause, the formal and the final cause. Attesting to the stability of human nature, the Roman philosopher Seneca spoke of "unwritten laws that are more certain than written ones."[7] This observation speaks to the fundamental pattern of unfolding development that is pre-inscribed in our nature, as well as in the natures of other things.

Traditionally, the results of this further development have been consigned to what is termed "accidental" to the substantial nature of the thing, but this can be misleading. The term "accidents" has suffered an emptying out of meaning in popular speech, and nowadays is more or less restricted to unforeseen disasters and financial settlements, as in accident insurance. In its etymology, however, the term refers to that which comes to, or rather comes about in, the stable center comprising the permanent core of a thing (cf. *per-maneo, permanens,* meaning dwelling throughout change). If I receive a medical education and undertake a practice, this does not render me human or non-human; I remain human at my core, and I remain a human being throughout.

But not all accidents are the same; some penetrate into the very substance of our humanity more than others, without altering the fact of our substantial identity. Now it is these intimate "accidental" qualifying characteristics that are of especial interest to both philoso-

7. "*Quaedam iura non scripta, sed omnibus scriptis certiora sunt.*" *Controversiae* I, 1, 14; Gallio speaking.

phers and psychotherapists, for—while they do not alter our right to be considered human—they do determine the concrete character of our humanity, e.g., the characteristics of gender and sexuality. I may undergo a sun tan with lighter consequences than my interest in art, or my compassion for the poor, or my capacity for generous friendship, or my tendency to anger or violence. Moreover, the consistency of my attitudes and behavior may well attest to the integration of such qualities into my actions, which, if repeated, become formative of my character. Not all so-called accidents are of equal value as contributors to the development of my humanity. Some accidents penetrate more deeply than others into the substance of my humanity. It is obvious that some developments and characteristics are more appropriate and more valuable than others. It is these that the philosopher appreciates and upon which the psychotherapist builds.

To understand the somewhat paradoxical character of nature, we need to distinguish the static from the permanent. When we consider something as static, we hold it against change in order to get a clearer, better view of it, as when we take a photograph, or a portrait painter freezes the momentary expression of a face. Such states are helpful and even necessary, but they are not the whole story. Heraclitus was not entirely wrong when he is said to have held that "all things change" *(panta rhei)*.[8] For natural things do change, perceptibly or imperceptibly; but many—even perhaps most—also retain an identity throughout the change. It is not a static identity but a permanent one that dwells throughout the change. With such an understanding of permanence and change, we can now once again take up the stable

8. Or more exactly that they are "in flux" *(rhoe)*. This is a somewhat one-sided and selective interpretation of Heraclitus's own view, furthered by Cratylus and Plato *(Cratylus* 402a) and only actually given this form by Simplicius *(Physics* 1313, 11). F. E. Peters, in *Greek Philosophical Terms* (New York: New York University Press, 1967), remarks: "As far as the technical language of philosophy was concerned [referring to Plato's use of the more balanced 'genesis' and Aristotle's use of 'kinesis'], *rhoe* [flux] was never more than a striking image" (p. 178).

yet dynamic concept of nature, as the source of the more or less permanent identity inherent in both men and things.

To recover and restore a stronger sense of human nature, it is helpful to translate the ontological language of the transcendental properties of being into the anthropological language of human dynamics and inclinations. In arguing that all things tend towards God as the fullness of being, Thomas, in Book III of his *Summa contra Gentiles,* cites Aristotle's principle:

> The reason of this is that all things desire and love existence; but we exist in activity, since we exist by living and doing; and in a sense one who has made something exists actively, and so he loves his handiwork because he loves existence. This is in fact a fundamental principle of nature; what a thing is potentially, that its works reveal in actuality.[9]

Thomas, however, widens the context, elevating the observation into a first principle:

> Things give evidence that 'they naturally desire to be,' so that if any are corruptible, they naturally resist corruptives, and tend to where they can be safeguarded.

And he adds:

> All things have being in so far as they are like God, Who is self-subsistent being, since they are all beings only by participation.[10]

In more contemporary language, reflecting the work of modern anthropology, John Bowlby cites the work of Geoffrey Gorer that summarizes the effects of these inclinations of human nature:

> All recorded human societies speak a language, conserve fire, and have some sort of cutting implement; all recorded societies elaborate

9. See the Loeb translation by H. Rackham (1972) of the *Nichomachean Ethics* (ix, 7, 4, 1168a). Cf. also the translation under the editorship of W. D. Ross in the *Student's Oxford Aristotle* (1942) at 1168a5, and also 1170a.

10. *Contra Gentiles* III, 19: "In rebus evidenter apparet quod 'esse appetunt naturaliter': unde et si qua corrumpi possunt, naturaliter corrumpentibus resistunt, et tendunt

the biological bonds of bearer, begetter, and offspring into kinship systems; all societies have some division of labour based on age and sex; all societies have incest prohibitions and rules regulating sexual behaviour, designating appropriate marriage partners, and legitimizing offspring; and all societies have rules and ritual concerning the disposal of the dead and the appropriate behaviour of mourners.[11]

As we reflect upon the actual conditions that prevail in the promotion and sustenance of human life, certain vital needs become evident. Among them the primary and governing need is the conservation of life, directly that of the individual, more expansively that of the collective, and ultimately of the race. For underlying the preservation of life can be seen indirectly the preservation of existence as the fundament of life, somewhat as light is seen in seeing color.[12]

This original and fundamental need of preservation finds its origin and its finality in the ultimate value of existence, that primary value recognized by the transcendental property of being *(esse, actus essendi)*, Hamlet's "to be or not to be." The conservation of existence, for human beings, entails the nurture and development of our essential humanity.

From this there follows a series of needs resident and active in our essential nature. There is the need for the physical means of conservation and development: the need for food and shelter. By extension this leads to the larger need to preserve and even to optimize the

illuc ubi conserventur. . . . Secundum hoc autem esse habent omnia quod Deo assimilantur, qui est ipsum esse subsistens: cum omnia sint solum quasi esse participantia." Thomas extracts the observation of Aristotle *(Nicomachean Ethics* IX, 7, 1168a5) concerning self-preservation and elevates it to a general principle pertinent to all caused beings.

11. Bowlby, *Loss, Sadness, and Depression,* vol. III of *Attachment and Loss* (New York: Basic Books/Perseus Group, 1980), p. 126. The citation is from Geoffrey Gorer's, "Death, Grief and Mourning in Britain," in *The Child in His Family: The Impact of Disease and Death,* ed. E. J. Anthony and C. Koupernik (New York: J. Wiley, 1973), pp. 423–24.

12. "When one sees colour one by the same act sees light, though one can see light without seeing colour. So, too, one can act with the recognition of particular means and at the same time with being in mind, or act for the sake of being without consideration of particulars. That is, being is fundamental and omnipresent in all acts" *(Summa theologiae* I-II, q. 8, a. 3, ad 2m).

overall conditions for physical survival and well-being, for *esse* and *bene esse*. This eventually entails the promotion of ecologically appropriate measures to ensure a healthy environment, which is obvious in the immediate environs but only now growing in awareness in planetary scope.

Closely associated with the need for physical goods is the need for security and safety, and ultimately for peaceful co-existence. These correlated human needs provide a sense of the unity of nations, races, groups, and individuals, in clear acknowledgment of the interrelated unity of our shared humanity. The notion of shared humanity may seem hopelessly remote and general from the actual conditions of human life today, and yet the Declaration of Human Rights is an expression of this transcendental unity. Implicit in that call for the transcendental unity of the species and the need for its preservation, there is the need built into our humanity that expresses the relationality of being *(aliquid)*. This interpersonal relationality acknowledges that the well-being of each of us and our associations cannot be sustained by an exaggerated, isolated individualism.

So far we have indicated the needs of our common humanity in terms of four transcendental properties of being: the actuality of our vital presence *(esse)*, the shared interests of our common humanity (essence), the interplay of unity and relationality *(unum et aliquid)*. These needs are—in their different ways—common to other forms of life as well, but they take on specific characteristics in the human species.

With the remaining transcendental features of being, however, it is as though the ontological heavens have opened up before us. For a new value, already implicit in the fabric of nature, discloses itself as the intelligibility and meaningfulness of being. It is the value of truth *(verum)*. With truth, as we shall see, a spiritual dimension makes its entrance into created, caused being, for with it the infinitude and inexhaustible light of being discloses itself.

Indeed, the light of truth already manifests a further value: that of the goodness of being *(bonum)*. This engages a second response to the texture of being: the first response engages the intellect in the discernment of truth; the second engages the will in the pursuit of the good as perfective.[13] In all of this explosion of being, the aura of its luminosity seals being with the transcendental feature of beauty *(pulchrum)*. With this brief rehearsal, we have revisited the texture of being and its transcendental features or properties in terms of our common humanity.

That humanity has been endowed with what St. Thomas has reflected upon as the inclinations of our human nature. It is these that make up the dynamic stability of our shared being and our common human nature. It is these that form the basis for culture and the ethics of natural law, and we need to take a closer look at the very concept of inclination as the initial bearer of natural law, culture, and society. For it is by way of the inclinations embedded in our shared nature, and through that nature ultimately grounded in the texture of being, that we find the ontological highway to the good life, to what Martin Seligman has termed the "strengths and virtues" that are "ubiquitous . . . [and] valued in virtually every culture."[14]

Here again, St. Thomas provides resources for our reflection. He remarks that there are inclinations embedded in human nature that give a prior direction towards our fulfilment. These directives unfold in three moments or stages: First, they are originally given with our nature and embedded in it as dynamic principles, the result of our coming into being by way of effective causality *(causa efficiens)*, with

---

13. "Every action, insofar as it possesses something of being, so far does it have goodness. But insofar as the action lacks some goodness to the degree proper to human action, so much does it lack goodness and is said to be evil" (*Summa theologiae* I-II, q. 18, a. 1). Also, stressing the ineradicable primordiality of the good: "Evil acts by virtue of a lack of good. For if, there were nothing in it of the good, neither would there be anything of being, nor would action be possible." (*Summa theologiae* I-II, q. 18, a. 1, ad 1m). And, marking the distinction between what I have called the texture of being and the mixture of reality: "Nothing prevents something to be in act [actual] in one respect, and deprived of act in another, causing a deficient action" (ibid., ad 2m). And finally: "An evil action is able to have a primary effect [*per se*], insofar as it has goodness and being."

14. *Authentic Happiness* (London: Nicholas Brealey, 2003), p. 102.

the imprint of the endowing agent or agents upon us: our parents and their lineage, but also the original cause of the very existence of that lineage.

Now, that origin carries with it an intended goal, the fulfilment of the potentialities embedded in our origin, so that the originating moment is predetermined in a general way by the moment of anticipated fulfilment and maturity *(causa finalis)*.[15] These two moments are realized by the guiding principle which is the directive or directives required for the realization of our humanity: the formal structure *(essentia)* and the dynamism of human nature *(causa formalis)* that realizes that structure. What the tradition calls "natural law" is the primordial directive of our shared humanity, by which we are enabled to realize the fulfilment—in innumerable and often surprising ways—of our shared formal and essential nature.

The normative guidance of beings in accord with their nature is more easily seen and can be formulated as a set of empirical laws, and where possible in mathematically precise terms. This has been the basis for the astounding success of the natural and positive sciences, which give an account in terms of formal laws.

In the case of final causes, however, the task is more difficult and less clear. That is why, no doubt, Francis Bacon advised that we restrict the play of final causality to human purposes and deny its application to subhuman nature. But even among humans, it is not easy to determine the appropriate end. If I see a bird in flight and have some knowledge of aeronautics, I can render an empirical explanation in terms of motion and gravity. I can say what the bird is *doing*. Still, that is not the whole story, for it does not render the full intelligibility of the event. If I ask *why* it is flying in a certain direction, I may—on the basis of past observations—say that it is because it is flying to its nest. But notice: the formal cause in itself is formulated on an actual ac

---

15. I will return in the final chapter to a discussion of this controversial and difficult concept of finality, which is too easily dismissed by the positivism inherent in the scientific method.

complished performance going on before our eyes: the bird is in actual flight; it is that *kind* of being. The finality of that performance, its final causality, however, is not observable but anticipatory. In this particular case I may have seen the nest, noticed the direction, and been familiar with the bird's habits, so that all is clear. But the final cause in itself and as such is not observable. It may be said that the formal law of flight is not seen as such either, but the law is being actualized before my eyes, whereas the finality is exercising its role in an embedded and anticipatory way. This is no doubt why the positive sciences speak of *drives* rather than of ends, since the notion of drives stresses the originating causality that impels the bird, rather than the anticipatory end of the motion. When St. Thomas speaks of inclinations, however, he means to embody finality (anticipation, directedness, and, in conscious beings, motive) as well as origin and law in the full account of the motion. The very intelligibility of directed motion demands completion through the principle of directed movement, i.e., through final causality, despite the positivist methodological suppression of such causality.

And indeed, the therapist seeks the path to the health and maturity of the patient through the difficult, complex, and perhaps surprising maze of the patient's individual and personal history. For health and maturity constitute the final cause and goal of the therapy.

⌢

In these two chapters I have sought to set forth the amazing complexity that enters into the constitution of each of us as individual human beings. Each of us manifests the texture of being, in which the principles of being and its transcendental properties are in play, not as a collection of separate facets but in the rich and concrete unity that seals the identity of each of us as human beings. We are far from simple in our complex participation in those very energies and modalities that are in play in each of us in remarkably unique ways: that make up the unique texture of our shared membership in the community of beings, that specify us as participating in our own way with our own kind in that formal principle that signs us as possessing human nature. So far the texture of our being.

All too obviously in play as well is what I have called the mixture of reality, those clouds and shadows that are part of the reality of the make-up of each of us. There is, first of all, our finitude, those limitations that mark us as limited participants in the rich texture of being. These are simple negations, which are also the very condition of our being as finite members of the community of being. To repeat, the very possibility of our identity marks us with the simple limitation of our finitude.

All too evident, as well however, are—not the simple negations—but the privations, which show that we are not all that we might be and might become, that mix of reality within which the texture of being shines with its positive values. It will not surprise you or offend you, if I remark that none of us is all that we might be, can be, and even ought to be.[16] But there is more to the story of who we are: notice, *who* we are, and not only *what* we are. And this is the story of our personhood to which we come in the next chapter.

What we have been given in our constitution is much, for it is the very compass of human development towards maturity that comes to us in the texture of our being and the specific inclinations of our nature. For the compass that is directive toward maturity is not rooted in the primacy of the ego and its method, but in values already resident in being and open to us, not by Cartesian or Kantian a priori filters, nor by an a posteriori empiricism, but by the ontological inheritance received in and through our nature and its inclinations. In Descartes' thought one reaches objects through the control of the method, and in Kant's thought, phenomena are constituted by the a priori forms of space and time and the categories of the understand-

---

16. Can be: I am here considering what maturity might mean within the parameters of our given nature. Christian revelation offers each of us unparalleled excellences beyond our power that are effected, not by what we *can* do, but by the grace of Redemption offered to us by the Author of our being and of all being.

ing. The tendency in much of modern thought is to take the ego—or some other form of consciousness, such as will in Nietzsche—as the first and decisive principle. As we expand our view, however, and situate ourselves in the context of being and the community of beings, we find that we participate in the texture of being with its transcendental properties and through the constitution of our specific nature with its inborn inclinations. It is these, and a new dimension, with which the psychotherapist deals and which discloses the transcendent reality of the person.

Such a psychotherapist will deal with the variations in personality, character, background, and values in each individual, but in the deeper context of human nature, whose inclinations already indicate a pathway to health, a pathway underlying the remarkable diversity of personal, familial, cultural, and social factors that offer themselves to the therapist.

By the light and energy of the transcendentals, those great luminaries of being, and by following the path of the inborn inclinations of our human nature, the therapist aids the patient in the recovery of health and the development towards maturity, even though the narrative, diagnosis, and remedy may never speak these words. For as members of the community of beings, we participate in the very texture of being, and we participate in its truth and goodness, through the inclination of our human nature as well as through the freedom we exercise as persons—to which we will now turn.

three

THE HUMAN BEING AS PERSON

After tracing out the dynamic inclinations of our human nature our story does not come to an end, for we are not only human beings; precisely as individual human beings we are persons. Now, a person is not simply the contraction from the specific and general character of our humanity to the particular instantiation of that specific character, as though our story ends with our membership in the species, or as when—colloquially—we mark our particularity with the idiomatic exclamation: "Oh! that's so personal!" Rather, our personhood marks in each of us the inner transcendence that characterizes our individuated human nature and gathers that nature up into a surpassing dimension in which intelligence and freedom are the sign and pathway of our destiny.

We know to our confusion that the person, elevated in concept and expectation, is often marred in reality. Once again, we must recall the distinction between the texture of being—to which the constitution of our personhood belongs and to which we are called—and the mixture of reality to which we too often succumb. As the history of the race shows, our humanity has descended too often into inhumanity (marring our essential nature), as division disrupts unity *(unum)* and deranges our innate relationality and community *(aliquid),* as we introduce falsity into truth *(verum),* evil into good *(bonum),* and the ugly into the beautiful *(pulchrum).* The texture of being survives these assaults, though, and provides the ground for a reasonable hope.

As our personhood takes up the inclinations of our nature, it lays upon us the task and the opportunity to retrieve that texture of being from the mixture of reality that we encounter in our factual condition. Both individually and as groups we live out this distinction between texture and mixture in the history of our race. From the study of early man, we can see the transcendent principle of personhood expressed in the early gathering and hunting societies, and in the early settlements with their organization of a societal life, the development of tools, the domestication of animals, the planting and harvesting of crops, the symbolic language of the cave paintings, the ritual magic and religious observances, the traditional story-telling, and the beginnings of political organization—all of these imprinting our distinctive presence upon the planet.

It is not, however until we come into possession of an explicit *concept* of the person that a new development in human self-understanding comes to expression. We can trace the origin of the concept and its self-understanding in the Mediterranean cultures of the second millennium before the present era, however else and wherever else it may have developed in other ways and in other cultures. From that Mediterranean culture we have received not only an insight into the person but the very word for it that is now in common use.

We may begin the story in Etruria, just north of Rome and Latinium, among the Etruscans. Through the religious cult dedicated to the goddess Persephone, they gave to the broader Roman language and culture the word *persona*, a fusion of the Etruscan *phersu* (mask) with the Latin word for 'sounding through' *(personare)*, thus associating the term with both language and manifestation. Among the Etruscans, the word named the mask worn by the portrayer of Persephone in the cult devoted to the goddess.[1]

Once translated into the Latin language and culture, the term underwent a remarkably diversified development, coming to designate the more general term for 'mask,' in the theater and in other contexts. Its use intensified, however, to come to stand, not only for the mask, but also for the personage disclosed by the mask. In grammar it named the different speakers, as in the first, second, third, and plural forms of address. In the political order it came to designate the citizen who alone had the full rights to participate freely in the councils of the city-state, no doubt reflecting the original dignity attached to the term, and distinguishing the male citizen from foreigners, women, children, and slaves, who did not enjoy this distinction (however shocking this is to us today). With this dignity came the rights and duties of property ownership and the right to initiate legal proceedings before a court of law, constituting its bearer as a juridical person. With Cicero it received a philosophical application, setting human individuals apart from other forms of life by distinguishing the individual human as a significant embodiment of the species, not wholly absorbed by that general membership.

A somewhat similar development of the term occurred in Greece, though the development reflected the more theoretical interest of that culture in contrast to the more practical developments in the Latin. The term *prosopon*, composed of the elements pros-, -op-, and -on, derived its central part from the verb "to see" (and its passive, "to be

1. For details see my article "The Geography of the Human Person," which originally appeared in *Communio* 13 (1986) and was subsequently reprinted in *The Texture of Being* (Washington, D.C.: The Catholic University of America, 2007), pp. 149–67, including fn. 1, which provides a brief bibliography of other publications from which I have drawn the history of the term.

seen"), and so it emphasized its association with the process of manifestation.[2] Now manifestation implies both surface and depth, fore-
ground and background, what is unveiled and what remains hidden.
This duality of light and shadow still reverberates in our contemporary use of the terms 'person' and 'personality', the latter referring
more to the visible effect of the person. Yet that visibility carried within it the distinctive interiority of the individual, as Aristotle noted in
asserting that the term *prosopon* stood for the human face, remarking
that "the part below the skull is named the face, but only in man, and
in no other animal; we do not speak of the face of a fish or of an ox."[3]

His remark is pertinent insofar as we often see in the faces of others the expression of an interior state of mind and feeling. I have written elsewhere that "a face is a structure that shows forth meaning. It
is transparent with the innocent, concealing with the devious, glow-
ing with the joyful, grieving with the sad, indifferent with the bored.
It is just this expressiveness upon which the actor and film star rely,
that the portraitist and photographer record, and towards which the
clown directs our attention. A person's face is meant to be the signature of the character within; one cannot disengage the face from a
certain interiority. A face has depth; it is not all surface. And yet that
depth is not a *thing* at all; (taken in its true character) it does not yield
to a scalpel. It is not [simply] the muscles or bones or brain, but a
depth that plays upon the surface of the countenance."[4] It is testimony
to the reality of the person that the diverse terms *phersu, personare,*
and *prosopon,* drawn from diverse cultures and contexts, have come
together in the word "person" to indicate the uniqueness, dignity, and
intimacy associated with our most distinctive mode of presence.

It was under a second religious impulse that the term gained new
life. In the Septuagint translation of the Bible, the phrase "out of the
mouth of the Lord" was rendered by the word *prosopon,* and the exe-
gete Philo Judaeus explained passages in the Wisdom literature using

2. The Greek variant, *prosopeion,* means "mask."
3. *Historia Animalium* 491b9–11.
4. *The Texture of Being,* p. 152.

the term "personification." The Latin translators used the term *persona (ex persona domini),* thus uniting the term and its concept with the Greek and the biblical usages.

Among the Christian Fathers of the early centuries and the Church Councils the term served to give expression to the intrinsic differential within the Triune Godhead between Father, Son, and Spirit, all one in the divine nature or essence, and thus was introduced an unprecedented distinction-within-unity. The term also served theologically to identify the Incarnate Christ as the union of two natures—divine and human—in the second Person of the Trinity, truly God and truly man. These two usages—Trinitarian and Christological—gave to the term 'person' a dignity which it has retained to this day; echoes of the *imago dei* have not been entirely lost, even in the modern process of secularization, for the term and concept took on new life in creative ways, being applied to all human beings as a distinctive name that took human nature and its inclinations up into a unity unlike that of other animal life. And so it has come to signify the highest dignity pertinent to each individual human being, as when we speak of personal rights and responsibilities.

⁀

Before proceeding to set forth the distinctive qualifying features of the human person through the properties of being, we need to remind ourselves that the term 'person' expresses not only those distinctive features but the entire individual human being as well. So that we use the term in two senses: precisely, to describe the distinguishing features of being human that differentiate the individual from other beings, as well as holistically, in order to designate the entire composite being who possesses those distinguishing features. In sum, the word serves to express what is distinctive and what comprehensive. We often use the adjective 'personal' to express the distinctive aspect, and the noun 'person' to encompass the whole being, traditionally expressed as the composite unity of body and soul.

In the first chapter I considered the ontological constitution of the person, and in the second the specific nature that places him or her

in a given category of beings, as expressed by the traditional defini-
tion of man as a rational animal. But focus upon the person in its holistic sense brings out a three-dimensional character of the individual human person that is of particular significance to the philosopher
and the psychotherapist. These three dimensions are simultaneously
at work in the actuation of our conscious life.

There is, first of all, the system of physical and biochemical forces operative within the individual. For the most part these forces fall
outside the realm of explicit consciousness.[5] They provide the person with the material basis for human life as a composite of body and
soul, mind and matter. The philosopher acknowledges this dimension
as the vital center that places the person in the context of material existence and the play of material energies and forces, subject in many
ways to the laws of motion common to all physical beings in the universe and, in a specific way, to living beings. This physical and vital dimension is of especial significance to the psychotherapist whenever
an individual patient is in need of medical assistance, either tempo-
rarily to stabilize a condition pertinent to his or her psychic and emotional state, or even permanently in the advancement of his or her
psychological health.

There is a second dimension intermediate between the person's
distinctive features and his corporeal and vital existence. It is a dimension that, since Descartes and the development of modern mechanism, is too easily reduced to mechanical forces, subject exclusively
to the laws of physical motion.[6] It may seem jejune to contradict such

5. Cf. A. Damasio, *The Feeling of What Happens*, pp. 142–43 and fn. 4, p. 347: "In
searching for precedents to the general idea that somehow the body is a basis for the
self, I have encountered it in Kant, Nietzsche, Freud, and Merleau-Ponty, although not
in the manner in which I articulate the idea with the tripartite arrangement of proto-
self, core self, and autobiographical self, and not with the emphasis on homeodynamic
stability." And further (p. 154; italics his): "I propose that the sense of self as a precon-
scious biological precedent, the *proto-self*, is a coherent collection of neural patterns
which map, moment by moment, the state of the physical structure of the organism in
its many dimensions. . . . We are not conscious of the proto-self."

6. Indeed, Julien Offray de la Mettrie wrote a work entitled *Man a Machine* (1748),

a view with the simple and everyday example of a pet dog, but let me risk your amusement. For the "patience" and "fidelity" of a pet animal, so remarked upon by animal lovers, disclose a disposition that, while not a human virtue, is also not a merely mechanical reaction. It is a lived disposition, fraught with both perception and emotion.

Nor does an explanation of such behavior in terms of the construction of images in the animal brain give an adequate account of the animal's action. For we have here a new dimension that transcends the play of merely physical forces. It is the medium of sensory perception and the feelings that attend it. We might best describe the relation of seeing to seen as a non-invasive relation, initiated by the perceiving animal (p. 40, "Relation and Interaction").

Taken precisely in itself, the relation does not alter anything in the object seen or heard, even though invasive action may follow upon the dog seeing his dinner or hearing the mailman. To be sure, the composite character of seeing involves a motion or process, but it is not only, nor even distinctively, that; seeing requires an agent, one who activates the process—one might say, a visitor to the production workshop capable of appreciating what has been produced.

It may seem demeaning to compare our sensory perception with that of a dog or other animals, but we do share this kind of sensory perception with them, and, in very different ways, the emotions that arise from it. It is precisely this that places the human in the genus of animal, even though we are—albeit often contrary to appearances and behaviors—carriers of a rational nature.

This sensory dimension is of interest, not only to the philosopher, but to the psychotherapist as well. For the latter does not address mechanical drives and reactions, as though repairing a machine, but engages a rich dimension of sensory perception and emotion in the

---

and materialism received further voice through d'Holbach, Marx, and others. Moreover, the reduction of the properly human to mechanistic forces is still common, since it seems to provide a clear and precise measure of human behavior. The reality, however, is at once more complex and richer than such a reduction allows.

Relation and Interaction

By a "non-invasive relation," I mean what is in contrast to a physical interaction. Although the instrumentality of the body plays a role in conveying the light needed for seeing, the sound-waves required for hearing, etc., the seeing transcends the exchange of energies. A contrasting view is that of A. Damasio (*The Feeling of What Happens*, p. 320); while vaguely aware that a deeper insight is obscured by the constraining presuppositions of his method, he writes that the term (used to describe knowing), "to represent" does not consist in replicating "the structure of the object." And further: "I do not have any idea about how faithful neural patterns and mental images are, relative to the objects to which they refer." This seems to dissolve the whole enterprise of scientific research. And, indeed, he adds: "But that does not mean that the image we see is the copy of whatever the object outside is like." And, then, in a recuperative attempt to recover the validity of representing, he remarks that what is represented in the end is not directly "the object but our interaction with the object insofar as it impacts upon the brain's activities." It seems hard, then, to see how Damasio can claim that we actually know—or even see—anything; and indeed, he does say that "whatever it [the "object outside"] is like, in absolute terms, we do not know." Notwithstanding, he claims that "the object is real, the interactions are real, and the images are as real as anything can be. And yet, the structure and properties in the image we end up seeing are brain constructions prompted by an object." The reality of the object, then, is confined to its role as a stimulus for the constructive activity of the brain. At first this may seem to be all that is needed for practical manipulation of the environment even if not for a theoretical understanding of it, even if we were to posit that the "object" (whatever it is) would stimulate us in the same way. But even that, over the long haul, would seem to demand trustworthy access on our part to the way things really are, at least to the way they act which is due to the way they are. Even if, as human, we are all in the same movie house, does that mean that we are seeing anything real, or simply a fictive, i.e., fictional, movie? As he remarks: "Since you and I are similar enough biologically to construct a similar enough image of the same thing, we can accept without protest the conventional idea [should we not read: belief?] that we have formed *the* picture of some particular thing. But we did not" (321). Despite this, he offers his interpretation as somehow representing the scientific truth of the way such processes really are.

Surely, the long history of truth-seekers (as I record here) might issue just such a protest of incongruency?

Bowlby, Beyond Freud

I am not in any way suggesting that Bowlby would agree with the present analysis, since much of it lies outside the principles of his method, nor am I suggesting, on his part, any lack of appreciation for Freud's groundbreaking work; his comments on Freud, though, are suggestive. Noting that the origins of Freud's model lay with his teachers in the field of physics, he remarks that Freud's "model represents an attempt to conceptualise the data of psychology in terms analogous to those of the physics and chemistry current in the second half of the nineteenth century. Impressed especially by the use physicists were making of the concept of energy, and by the principle of conservation, Helmholtz held that, throughout science, real causes must be thought of as being some kind of 'force'.... Accordingly Freud, eager to frame his concepts in terms of a proper science, borrowed and elaborated a model that had been built with these concepts by Fechner ...." But Bowlby finds that "the psychical energy model is logically unrelated to the concepts that Freud, and everyone since, regards as truly central to psychoanalysis—the role of unconscious mental processes, repression as a process actively keeping them unconscious, transference as a main determination of behaviour, the origin of neurosis in childhood trauma. Not one of these concepts bears any intrinsic relation to a psychical energy model; and when this model is discarded all four remain intact and unchanged. The psychical energy model is a possible model for explaining the data to which Freud drew attention; it is certainly not a necessary one" (*Attachment*, pp. 15–16; the whole discussion on method is worthwhile, pp. 3–23). S. A. Mitchell, in a foreword to the 1999 edition of Bowlby's *Separation, Anxiety, and Anger* (p. x), sees a development in attachment theory: "Bowlby's concept of 'working models' had an overly schematic, mechanistic feel to it.... But the more recent attachment literature (Fonagy) has taken a more inward turn in exploring ... the texture of conscious and unconscious subjectivity."

context of conscious human life. Ancient thought captured this dimension with the concept of the animate soul and the theory of sensory powers, and it detailed the sensory appetites and emotions with considerable insight (see above, "Bowlby, Beyond Freud").

At this level there is an aspect of particularized sensory meaning experienced, even by animals, and reinforced by memory and expectation based upon past experience. Once again, it is a distortion to reduce such sensing to a mechanical operation, consisting entirely of the play of physical forces or drives; for when an animal, including a human animal, sees, hears, smells, it acts, is an agent, and thereby it experiences a non-invasive relation in association with the objects to which it responds. Invasive action may follow upon such an association but the association itself, the relation as such, is non-invasive. Looking at something doesn't alter the thing looked at.

There is more to sensory knowing than the production of images, since pictures imprinted in the nerve system of the brain, like pictures on a screen, do not account for the agent *seeing* them; it is likewise for hearing, smelling, or even touching them. There is something more occurring here, for sensing does not take place in an empty picture gallery, mere patterns in the brain. There is required a viewer in this gallery, and the viewer initiates a new dimension, a dimension not merely of having received or constructed a figure, but of having taken up that construct into a new mode of existence, the life of a perceiving animal, human or other.

All the brain chemistry in the world will not magically produce that visitor to the putative gallery, nor can the visitation be ignored if we are to give a full account of what actually happens.[7] For a new relationship is established, not simply a spatial relation between one thing (the sensing animal) and another thing (the physical object), nor even merely a chemical reaction, but a non-invasive relation that lives in a new dimension, that of sensory life.

No doubt, the sciences of motion have much to contribute to a fuller understanding of such sensory experience, since motion does

---

7. A. Damasio (*The Feeling of What Happens*, p. 11) resorts to the metaphor of the movie house as he points to two problems that seem to elude the neurobiology of consciousness: "How the movie-in-the-brain is generated, and the problem of how the brain also generates the sense that there is an owner and observer for that movie." The latter problem requires a shift of presuppositions and a broader context than the presuppositions of his method permit. Extending the metaphor (p. 21), he speaks of "mapping" different objects; but I don't see a map of the object, though the mapping may well be a means of my seeing it. Still, unless I am wholly and inescapably deluded, my experience tells me that I see the thing itself, not a map of it.

engage the whole being, body and consciousness, in both humans and the higher animals, and sensory experience does not occur without such an engagement; but what is necessary is not necessarily sufficient. To give a full account, we need to acknowledge the distinctive character common to the non-invasive medium of sense perception and emotion, and the involvement of agency as distinct from process.

⌒

We now move on to the next stage in our analysis: to the person. In the instance of the higher animals, such as the dog just mentioned, the non-invasive relation does not have the universal sweep of abstract thought associated with human intelligence. It is more restricted, indeed, restricted to the particular space-time situation. Sensory perception is a relation more or less confined to a particular spatial and temporal situation. I say, more or less, because past situations are retained in sensory memory and play their role through habituation in the determination of the response. Young animals may have to learn and remember what is to be feared or desired. Still, insofar as the non-invasive perception of an object is sensory, it does not reach to what the thing is apart from the participation in the particular situation—or other remembered situations—in which it is perceived. The animal perceiving gives no sign of being able to formulate its awareness in general linguistic and conceptual terms. The animal's perception does not reach to a comprehension of the nature of the thing in itself, distinguished from its particular space-time instantiation— whereas human intelligence provides a general name that expresses the universal concept which re-presents what the being is. It is upon such re-presenting, in yet another dimension, that the mind bases a conceptual understanding of the world of objects and things.

This new step towards a general mode of comprehension inaugurates what, speaking figuratively, I might express as an explosive moment. It is a moment that we have each and all experienced in our first years without retaining memory of it, but which has since become part of our daily lives. It is that moment when—inchoatively—

Discovery of Sign and Concept

There is at least one exception to the forgetfulness of the discovery of sign and concept, and that is the remarkable experience of Helen Keller, corroborated by her teacher. In her autobiography Helen recalls how, when she was a child, deaf and blind, her teacher pressed the sign for water into her hand as cool water splashed over her fingers. The connection between sign and thing was instantaneous, as was her response. She fell upon the ground, one hand clutching the teacher's, the other clutching objects, one after another, to demand from her teacher the sign (word) that named each. From that moment of the discovery of literacy, Helen developed into the fully intelligent and educated person she became. With the discovery of sign and concept, the dimension of human thought opened up to her.

the dimension of intellectual thought and experience opens up to us, disclosing a limitless horizon of intelligibility and meaning. Objects and things disclose themselves to us, once again in a non-invasive association, but this time without the restriction to particular space-time situations, experienced or recalled and joined together. It is the moment of truth, the food of human intelligence upon which it lives and grows. While things retain their own being, it is not too much to say that they offer themselves to us, that they make themselves available to us in an unprecedented way.

We often speak of the product of this moment as abstract, insofar as its fruits—concepts or ideas—are relatively empty. For when I say "dog" I simultaneously designate all dogs, and yet no one dog in particular. But this relatively empty generality that is proper to concepts contains within it the promise of a rich harvest, from which several quite astounding effects result.

First of all, we reach things, not simply in their restricted circumstances, nor even simply as objects, but as they are in their being. Indeed, that is what our study of the world, including the investigations of science, seeks to realize—though never exhaustively, since the search for further understanding continues.

Moreover, our thought does not stop at the level of abstract ideas, but goes on to judgments that rejoin us with the world as it is, as when we affirm that such and such is so and so. This makes us distinctive participants in the drama of being, bringing a new dimension of value, viz. truth-values, into play.

Nevertheless, the first stage of relative emptiness and abstraction is of decisive importance in a second way, since it releases us from the grip of particularity and opens us up to an unlimited horizon of intelligibility. That release is our ticket to freedom, for the universality of language and thought is the necessary condition for freedom of deliberation, choice and action, as the mind moves in deliberating possible alternatives. Within our composite nature, then, the person is liberated in consciousness from the restricted condition of our individual corporeity and our sensory particularity and invited to explore the depths and outer reaches of being; then it is within this open field of meaning and values that we find the roots of our freedom.

Before we consider the meeting of our intelligence and freedom with the pre-given inclinations of our nature, it will be well to consider briefly the distinctively transcendent character of the personal attributes of intelligence and freedom that are ensconced in that human nature. It is traditional to refer to these features as spiritual in character, inasmuch as they cannot be accounted for in terms of the physical forces that also play themselves out in our composite nature. It is not easy to set forth the distinctive character of these transcendent spiritual energies, given the prevailing reductive materialism so familiar to our culture; but it is possible at least to indicate and suggest the difference of these energies from the physical principles and forces that are also operative in our knowing processes, as well to distinguish the universal scope of intelligence from the more restrictive sensory associations that also form part of our conscious life.

By means of the spiritual character of our intelligence—at once non-invasive, initially abstract and universal—we find ourselves in the world in a quite distinctive way. Although what I will now say pertains in its own restricted and particular way to sensory experience as well as to intellectual cognition, let me directly address the intellectual relation in its proper character as abstract and universal. As we take our place in a room, we interact with the physical forces already operative in its space: breathing its air, pressing down on the floor and the seats with our bodies, exchanging our body heat, absorbing and reflecting the light rays, etc. Thus far, then, our bodily presence in the room.

But we are present in another way as well, in being aware of the room, its environs and objects. This distinctively intellectual mode of awareness exercises its presence in a radically different way from the physical reactions already mentioned. The physical interaction entails a bodily exchange, and if we have a finely enough tuned instrument we would be able to detect the fact of our having been present in the room, even after we had left it, through the residue of particles left in the recently vacated space. Unless we have left physical signs, however, such as a written note or some such indication, others would not normally know of this new mode of presence having inhabited the room—that is to say, that we have seen the objects in the room, understood their functions and significance, and been present to them in this distinctive way without physical interaction determining the essential character of that relation, though physical reactions to light rays and other forces will also have played an instrumental role in supporting this new mode of presence.

Insofar as we have simply understood the room and its objects, we do not alter the situation but leave it as we had encountered it. There is only one presupposition required to accept this analysis of understanding and its universal non-invasive medium. It is that we do indeed reach the truth about things as they are in their own being, however incomplete our grasp of them is. If this were not so, then all our attempts to gain a true understanding of things, including science's own investigations, would be a mockery and delusion.

As has already been said, in coming to know the room and its objects we are present to the room in a non-invasive way, and it is present to us in a way that does not compromise it in its own being. There is a new and distinctive way of the coming together of ourselves and the room under our initiative, though this agency is quite unlike the physical interaction that marks our bodily intervention in the room. It will be quickly pointed out that physical processes—the light in our eyes, the particles in the odors, the electro-chemical impulses in the brain—are at work and are necessary if this new mode of presence is to be realized; for human knowing is a total, composite human activity, engaging the full energy and formality of our nature. Nevertheless, within this complex there is a modality that is not physical, that is not accounted for in terms of physical motion and physical forces. In sum: this mode of non-physical presence is situated in the context of our composite human nature, so that the action of knowing is a fully human undertaking.[8] Together, these modes of being-present—physical and intellectual (as well as the previously analyzed sensory mode)—unite to form what was traditionally known as the substantial union of form and matter, of soul and body, and its operative actions.

To acknowledge such a radical dimension within the human composite one must transcend the exclusive preoccupation with the physical sciences, dedicated as they properly are to the investigation of motion. To someone dedicated to the empirical investigation of phenomena, it is neither easy to acknowledge, nor obvious, that the full nature of our human being can be understood only by recognizing the distinctive character of agency operative in this second modality within our composite being.[9]

8. The question understandably arises whether this spiritual dimension can survive death, i.e., the separation from its bodily base. For St. Thomas' discussion and demonstration of the immortality of the intellectual soul, see *Summa theologiae* I, q. 75, aa. 2 & 6, which address the questions, Whether the Human Soul is Subsistent, and Whether the Human Soul is Corruptible?

9. It might be remarked here that transcendence of the particularity of sensory-physical situations, as well as of restriction to empirical methods of investigation—as distinct from the present argument which is based upon cognitive experience—allows

On the other hand, if by its reductionist tendencies much of modern thought obscures the non-invasive character of human intelligence, it still testifies to the importance and distinctive worth of the person in the practical sphere, for modern thought will not do without the concept of person in those aspects of our society that it prizes, particularly in economics, politics, and social interaction. This is given expression most notably in the call for the respect of human rights. But much of modern thought in its positivist tendency, because of its presuppositions, avoids locating the root of this practical acknowledgment of personal values in the theoretical and transcendent character of the human person. The prevailing habits of mind have no methodological principles with which to take account of a spiritual mode of existence. Still, if we aspire to a fuller and deeper understanding of ourselves with the preoccupation that we give to understanding material forces, we are drawn into the recognition of the indispensable presence of this non-invasive principle operative within our human nature.

Now, this detachment from physical forces is the initial condition supporting our freedom, for it liberates us from confinement to the particularity of present and past situations. "Detachment" here is the art of abstraction that occurs in the initial formation of the meaning expressed in our words. It does "give birth" to a new dimension that is not physical or material. The "offspring" are the new words. In a certain sense this detachment transcends space and time insofar as it holds for all possible situations. Indeed, conception is aptly named, since the formation of concepts is quite literally a "giving birth in a new dimension"—and if I am permitted another metaphor: to new "offspring." And this comes about not simply as a motion, but

---

us to recognize that final causality is in play, whereas empirical methods deal with effective causality as initiating force and formal causality as design, but reductively translate final causality into motive force. See Bowlby's dismissive remarks regarding "the ghost of teleology" in *Attachment*, vol. I (New York: Basic Books/Perseus Group, 1969, 2nd ed. 1982), p. 51; also p. 111, fn. 1; and p. 124.

in and through actions that emerge from an individual being of a certain (human) kind. It is in and through such action that we penetrate to the very core of the thing.

As we look back at our reflection we summarize our given complexity as the union of three basic levels that constitute our nature and our person: the physical and biochemical factors that secure our existence, the non-invasive but particularizing sensory mode of consciousness that engages the physical world, and the non-invasive intellectual mode that opens us to intelligible horizons and provides the knowing foundation for our liberty.

It is just here that our reason and our liberty meet the pre-given inclinations embedded dynamically in our nature. Our knowing and our choosing "arise out of" and "point back to" the course of maturity and growth in our development.[10] But they let the path between be discerned and determined by the cooperation of our sensory and intellectual knowledge with our freedom. And, as we will see, it is just here that the development of the virtues comes into play.

These virtues are not simply moral perfections, but include all manner of developed capacities for the appreciation of the texture of being and the values—moral and others—that are constitutive of that structure. There are vital values affecting our health and survival, technical values permitting a judicious stewardship of our environment, aesthetic values that appreciate the luminous wonder of being, intellectual values that open us out to vast spheres of meaning, and religious values that acknowledge the sublime giftedness of being.

It is, however, the moral values, rooted fundamentally in the good of being and more proximately tailored to the specificity of our human nature, that most directly form us in the completion and maturity of our humanity, for these alone determine the value of the exercise of responsible freedom. It is just here that our freedom is called into the service of the perfection of our humanity. The other perfections

10. See the three-fold development of originating causality, formal causality, and final causality set out in the previous chapter as inclinations of our nature.

receive their definitive value in and through the use we make of our liberty, for it is in that use that we exercise the initiative that is exclusively human, action that bears our personal signature. To use a simple, almost banal example: to fail to develop a musical talent because of a defect in hearing is not a debit to us as persons; but to fail to develop it, though we have drawn upon the support of others, because of laziness is a personal defect, if not the most deleterious.

Here again, within the mixture of being and non-being that constitutes reality as distinct from the texture of being, in the mix of light and shadow, of benefit and privation, we find the remote foundations of the virtues in the texture of being and its transcendental properties. For within the inclinations of our nature there is embedded the promise of the future realization of our essential humanity *(essentia, res humana)*, the guarantee of our individuality, our oneness of being *(unum)*, and the hope of genuine community in our relationality (peaceful and productive co-existence, *aliquid*); in the honesty *(verum)* with which we probe the meaning of things (their intelligibility), and face the trials and disappointments of our adversity, as well as the joy of understanding one another and the world we encounter, finding in it a deeply seated good *(bonum)* in being alive, in concert with others, in an environing world; able to appreciate its astonishing beauty *(pulchrum)*. All of these transcendental properties of being provide the ground for the development of our humanity. It is our responsibility to recognize the texture of being as well as the mix of reality within which it is ensconced, using the transcendental properties of being as the ground for the development of virtue and maturity.

But the realization of our maturity occurs in the world of practical life, and so we need to conclude this—up to now theoretical—reflection on the person with a consideration of *praxis*, the practical life.

We have come a long way in setting forth the inner constitution of the human person. We find within the person as participant in the texture of being a directive compass consisting of the transcendental properties of being; in the constitution of our human nature, in the distinctively spiritual character with its non-invasive agency, along with the sensory powers and the physical energies that all together define the specific nature which each person shares with others, we find operative the essential and directive inclinations of our common humanity. But it is precisely in the spiritual openness brought about by consciousness that we find the pathway to the person's liberty, which allows a free engagement with what is encountered; and finally, it is the will to act that carries us into the domain of practice and action and the self-development of the person in community with others and in engagement with things.

It is just here that I have found in the philosophical writings of the Polish philosopher Karol Wojtyła (better known as Pope John Paul II) a shift of emphasis that is fruitful. Among those who are cognizant of contemporary philosophy, Karol Wojtyła is best known as a phenomenologist, the practitioner of a mode of reflection initiated largely by Edmund Husserl at the beginning of the last century and as a corrective to the prevailing materialism endemic to the thought of the time, as it continues to be today. In winning his doctorate in philosophy at the University in Cracow after the Second World War, Wojtyła adapted the work of the phenomenologist Max Scheler to his own purpose,[11] which was to examine the inner life of consciousness and its relation to the possibility of a Christian ethics. This topic already placed the weight of his thought in the scales of human action.

As he began teaching at the Free University of Lublin in 1954, however, he turned back to the mediaeval period in order to appropriate the metaphysical tradition of Plato, Aristotle, Augustine, and Thomas as providing a foundation and grounding for a more comprehensive sense of human action and the human person than phenomenology alone could provide.

---

11. See his doctoral dissertation, *On the Possibility of Constructing a Christian Ethic on the Basis of the System of Max Scheler* (Lublin: TNKUL, 1959); available in German and Spanish translations.

In the *Lublin Lectures* he sets forth a metaphysics of being that is drawn from these traditional thinkers.[12] At the same time, while retaining the metaphysics of being as the comprehensive foundation of the human person, he reflects upon the developments that have occurred in the seven centuries since St. Thomas Aquinas brought that metaphysics to a rich state of development. Sensitive to the modern currents of thought, and to the accumulation of human power during those seven centuries, especially in the acquisition of modern science and modern technology, he takes up the question of the nature of human action *(actus humanus)*.

Some years later (in 1969) he published his major philosophical reflection on the philosophy of the person *(Osoba i Czyn)*, known in its English version under the title *The Acting Person*.[13] In this philosophical work he reflected upon the inner life of consciousness while retaining the traditional metaphysical horizon within which the human being takes up his or her life of personal consciousness within the wider community of beings. In shifting the emphasis to action, Wojtyła takes account of the contribution of phenomenology to an understanding of the interior life of the person as agent, but he corrects its latent idealism by grounding the analysis within the traditional—principally Thomistic—metaphysics of existential act. Current idealism makes the intentional relation of the mind to the object central and definitive for the character of consciousness and the person, thus absolutizing consciousness in the tradition of modern idealism.[14] This has the effect of imprisoning consciousness and its ob-

12. *Wykłady lubelskie* (Lublin: TNKUL, 1986). Translated only into German, *Lubliner Vorlesungen* (Stuttgart: Seewald Verlag, 1981).

13. *Osoba i Czyn* (Polskie Towarzysto Teologiczne, 1969); translated into English by A. Potocki, revised by Anna-Teresa Tymieniecka, under the title *The Acting Person* (Dodrecht, Holland: Reidel, 1979). The most up-to-date version is the Polish-Italian third edition, *Persona e Atto*, ed. G. Reale and T. Styczen (Milan: Rusconi Libri, 1999), which is not yet available in English.

14. My teacher in Germany, Eugen Fink, a student of Husserl, concluded that his respected and beloved teacher had indeed taken the turn in his later works *(Cartesian Meditations, Parisian Lectures)* towards an idealism that presumably may have been

jects within itself or its relation to its constituted objects, thus erecting consciousness, in the manner of idealism, into an absolute center of what it means to be a person.

Instead, Wojtyła relativizes the role of intentionality, acknowledging the part it plays in the presentation of objects to consciousness. But the essential character of consciousness lies elsewhere. For while conscious and non-conscious powers—physical and sensory—play their role in constituting the object within the "field of consciousness," the known does not become appropriated to the inner life of the mind as known until it is reflected in the non-invasive, spiritual dimension that is resident and active within the whole human person as a composite being, not merely as a consciousness. As Aristotle had already insisted, it is not the mind that knows but the person by means of the mind. This de-centering of intentionality liberates both consciousness and the things it encounters in experience to be themselves, thus restoring the basic horizon of the community of beings and the fundamental horizon of metaphysics within which the human person exercises his or her conscious and active life.

What Wojtyła calls reflective consciousness, which translates the objects of cognition into the dimension proper to consciousness, also discloses the role of consciousness as the participant in this translation, and in so doing it thus discloses consciousness to itself, so that the action when properly human *(actus humanus)* is self-conscious.

This self-conscious awareness does not stop with the consciousness of itself as the initiator of the knowledge of objects and of itself, but penetrates more intimately within the sphere of consciousness to the very center and core of personal life itself. And here Wojtyła finds the ultimate source of human action and the distinctive character of the person to reside in his or her freedom. In possessing the freedom to act, the human person (as agent) is called to act upon the

latent in his earlier work. Others, of course, disagree, and there can be no doubt that Husserl's phenomenology, in opening up the intentional field of objects, was an answer both to the prevalent scientific materialism and to the Cartesian-Kantian idealism.

knowledge available to him or her, and so the self is always ingredi-ent in conscious human action (as distinct from mere reaction), for in acting upon the knowledge available to the self, the conscious person is self-possessed, self-governed, and self-determining.

This triple capacity calls for the integration of the physical condi-tion, the drives, emotions and cognitions in possession of the self; fur-ther, however, it also initiates the dynamic transcendence with which the person moves beyond the present condition either via the texture of being to an increase in its humanity, or in the mix of non-being to its lessening. It is just here that the psychotherapist is engaged in as-sisting that development. And it is to this that we now turn.

four

＞

PSYCHOTHERAPY AND PHILOSOPHY

Their Common Border

It is time to bring my philosophical reflections into closer engagement with the psychological literature that I have been reading and which has directed the previous chapters in a quiet and subliminal way. Since I am not a psychologist, you will not expect of me a detailed discussion of the research that forms the basis of my remarks, but I hope that these remarks reflect my appreciation for the contribution that psychoanalysis and psychotherapy have made to our understanding of what it means to be human and to be a person.

Let me draw your attention to five touch points from which this philosopher finds food for thought from psychotherapy, thought about the rich complex that is the human person. It is not my intention to minimize the contribution of psychopathology to the curative well-being of persons, but I will attend principally to the contributions made by positive psychology to what is required in the development of human and personal health.

To this end, let me consider the five touch points: (1) the *physiology* and the non-conscious processes constantly at work in the life of the person; (2) the *emotional-affective* dynamisms that provide much of the conscious basis for evaluative human moods and emotions; (3) the *sensory-perceptive* outreach of the human organism in its immediate and particular contact with its surrounding world; (4) the *intellectual* and *cognitive* openness of the person to being and to beings beyond itself; (5) and finally, the attainment of voluntary action in freedom. In sum: the non-conscious, emotion, perception, cognition, and liberty.

Let me remark a bit more upon the difference in the method employed in psychological research and the reflection undertaken by philosophy. Any method serves to direct the mind to certain selected data, but it also excludes other data outside its focus. It is paradoxical that the very restriction of interest that attends each special method enlarges our understanding of the subject under investigation. Thus, the empirical tests of psychological research have enriched our knowledge of the human person in a way that the intellectual effort of philosophical reflection on the powers of the soul could never do and has not in its more than two millennia of practice ever done.

At the same time, philosophical reflection addresses issues that lie outside psychological interest, touching upon a broader, if vaguer, all-encompassing horizon and open to the original depths of existing beings. Indeed, the very term "precision"—so valued in research, so absent in non-Cartesian philosophy,[1]—tells us much. The mediaeval

---

1. St. Thomas Aquinas draws an important distinction between "abstraction" and "*praecisio.*" Abstraction withdraws from particular instances in favor of a universal conception of general kinds, but it remains open to those same particular instances, as "man" awaits its instantiation in "this" man; whereas "praecisio" deliberately excludes reference to anything but the essential core content of the concept, to consider the "*quidditas tantum,*" the universal in exclusion from all particularization (see *De Ente et Essentia*). By extrapolation, the empirical methods of modern science attain their great success by the exclusion of all but selected aspects of the data under investigation. Much of modern philosophy, in imitation of the special sciences, and after the manner

Latin term meant "to cut off or exclude," as when a surgeon makes an "incision." It stood in contrast to the term "abstraction" which means "withdrawal," as when I refer to our common "humanity" without reference to our concrete and particular differences, yet leaving room for them to be considered, not excluding them as in "precision." It is precision that has cut such a rich and detailed harvest of meaning and understanding in modern psychological research, as well as more generally in the positive and empirical sciences.

Now, putting such a high and precious value on precision is a pervasive characteristic of much of modern thought, a value that has brought what philosophy could never bring to the armada of enquiry. It is my view, however, that so exclusionary a method is not appropriate for philosophy, which searches out the broadest expanse of things and their most fundamental depths, even if with modest success. It was, above all, Descartes who refashioned philosophy in the pursuit of "clear and distinct" ideas—clear, so that nothing obscure or incomplete was left to be said about a given idea, and distinct, in the sense that the idea in its intelligible outlines excluded all others and was separate and separable from them. No doubt Descartes reflected the growth of the positive sciences in their quest for exact and testable understanding to match the growing demand for technological control.[2] In so doing he set a standard and expectation for what might count as certain and certified scientific knowledge, even if he failed to meet that criterion in some of his own thought.

Yet the ideal of precision has broad influence and appeal even

---

of the Cartesian "filtering out" of all that is not "clear and distinct," has adapted the exclusionary method, whereas earlier traditional philosophy, for the most part, pursued a focus that sought to embrace—from its point of interest in the most comprehensive intelligible way—being as such, the entire horizon of entitative reality and its constitutive principles, while remaining open to their concrete embodiment in reality.

2. It is significant that Descartes defined acceptable ideas (as clear and distinct), but considered freedom of the will to be without limit (*Meditations* IV), and that he pointed to the practical sciences of mechanics and medicine as the sought for fruits of the tree of knowledge.

among those who reject Descartes' precise separation of mind and body. I don't think I am wrong in finding that certain psychological investigators who hold an understandable and correct aversion to Cartesian dualism and the famous—or infamous—mind-body problem, at the same time prize the high value of precision. Thus, John Bowlby remarks that few today would be satisfied with the purely Cartesian dualism of mind and body, or—for that matter—on the other side, with the epiphenomalist (and even materialist) reduction of psychic phenomena to "the physical world as alone real," which follows from the rejection of Cartesian dualism.[3] (The epiphenomenalist view considers thought and feelings to be "no more than shadows, playing no real part in life's drama," and therefore reduced to the scientifically irrelevant.) And yet, as I will argue, Bowlby's own method is closer to Cartesian clear and distinct ideas than he would likely admit.[4]

There is a general tendency towards treating the unity of the human person in its individuality as a unity of function among discrete parts, those parts being often related in certain spheres, such as the brain, to a principal part. This is to treat the unity of the person mechanistically and atomistically, a way of treatment prepared by nominalism, in which the relations are external to one another and the unity is that of a resultant organized system, or a system of systems. But this sort of unity derives from the demand for precision that is imposed by the method in search of definitive clarity and precision. The method bypasses the organism as possessing a holistic principle of its own that effects an internal unity of the whole. Philosophy, as I understand

3. *Attachment and Loss*, vol. I: *Attachment* (New York: Basic Books/Perseus Group, 1969, 2nd ed. 1982, reprint 1999), p. 106.

4. By "Cartesian" here I refer to Descartes' precise, methodical filtering of the full being and meaning of the realities he encountered through the a priori rules of his method, so as to accept as beyond a doubt only those ideas that were so clear and distinct that they did not yield to the doubt. It was, however, the idealized properties of mathematical intelligibility and meaning that alone survived the filter and determined what was meant by "clear and distinct" (*Discourse on Method*, Parts II & IV). The question to be asked, of course, is whether reality is to be identified exclusively with its mathematical properties.

it, proposes a more holistic method of reflection that transcends precision in order to do justice to the rich unity and totality of the entity as such and not simply the order of its parts, a method in which the ontological values of the entity in its being are acknowledged as constitutive of its unity in a way that completes and overrides its parts. So there is this paradox: The detailed richness of the human person, disclosed by detailed psychological research, is unavailable to philosophical reflection on its own, but philosophy seeks a more holistic understanding, not by ignoring the detail or positively excluding it, but by seeking to encompass it and ground it.

Finality plays a role in this holistic endeavor, by providing a distinctive unity. The mechanistic approach, which is taken to be obvious operationally in much of the research, has rejected final causality as an intelligible principle. Bowlby refers to it as "the ghost of teleology."[5] This is not unusual. The effect of several thinkers who played a decisive role in shaping modern thought also found the principle to be of little use in their endeavors. Thus, already in the seventeenth century, Descartes, Hobbes, and Spinoza denied its efficacy, while Francis Bacon allowed it for purposive human actions only. Moreover, those who were developing the modern science of motion in physics found it of little relevance to their search for mathematically formulable laws. It subsequently has found little support or use, even in the social sciences. And yet the very notion of orientation intrinsic to the concept of natural inclination—on which we base our expectation of predictable and repeated behavior—implies it.

Still, final causality is a difficult and obscure concept—especially as operative prior to purpose, since motive and motivation (as distinct from adaptation) must be distinguished from motor force. To ascribe and restrict finality to human purpose may not be difficult, though even that ascription is problematic with many thinkers if not simply denied; yet to understand it as necessary for a fuller comprehension of non-human dynamism—and of all caused being—is for-

5. Bowlby, *Attachment*, p. 51.

Adaptation and Finality

John Bowlby, in *Attachment*, says: "There are many reasons why the concepts of adaptation and adaptedness give rise to difficulty. One is that the words themselves—adapt, adapted, adaptation—carry more than one meaning. A second is that in biological systems the condition of being adapted is achieved by unusual means, an understanding of which is constantly hindered by the ghost of teleology" (p. 51). Referring (p. 111, fn. 1) to the work of M. B. Arnold (*Emotion and Personality*, 2 vols. Vol. I: *Psychological Aspects* [New York: Columbia University Press, 1961]), Bowlby remarks that "some of her formulations are flawed by teleology." But one may well ask whether Bowlby has a correct understanding of the concept, for he complains: "Such a theory entails supposing that the future determines the present through some form of 'final causation' [which] lies outside the realm of science. As such, finality is not compatible with 'hard science'" (p. 125). Moreover (p. 69), he replaces the term "goal directed" with the term "set-goal", because it better describes the outcome, rather than the object, e.g., the interception of the prey (i.e. the action of the subject or agent), rather than the role of the victim (i.e. the object or final cause). In this way Bowlby's analysis remains within the methodological requirements of control systems theory. And further (at p. 124): "If we are not to be trapped in theories of a teleological kind, it is necessary to walk warily.... [We need to] discover how to express the concerns of the vitalists in the exact scientific language of the mechanists." For all that, as noted in the previous chapter, Bowlby's use of mechanism is qualified: he observes that Freud imported the model of physical force into psychoanalysis rather than deriving it from the practice of psychoanalysis itself, modeling it rather on nineteenth-century physics and chemistry, whereas "the psychical energy model is logically unrelated to the [physical] concepts that Freud, and every one since, regards as truly central to psychoanalysis." He adds that "Freud's energy model originated outside psycho-analysis"; he asks (rhetorically) "whether there may by now be an alternative better suited for the purpose in hand" (pp. 15–16).

bidden to a mechanistic method that relies for its explanations upon effective causality alone. Finality understood as motivation, though, is not an effective force pressing itself upon a thing to displace it either by an internal force or by an external mover, nor even by an attractive force (after the manner of a magnet). Finality is, rather, an ingrained tendency and orientation that is present within the motion and the mover as determining it to this rather than to that outcome. In effective motor causality, one can separate out the moving cause, as a being external to another being or as an internal part acting upon another part propelling it. To speak colloquially, however, finality does not provoke, it prompts; it does not effectuate, it orientates.

Ordinary usage overrides the restriction of the scientific method in acknowledging that it is natural for a given thing to do this or that by appealing to an internal motivation rather than to an extrinsic force. When we say that a thing has functioned "better," we appeal to a latent measure inscribed into the thing's nature, though not as a material element or component, and that influences it *before* it has been actualized or realized. Finality is an intelligible orientating principle—not an actual force—that is embedded in the form of the thing's nature yet is in relation to another, as yet unrealized, good. The scientific denial of the principle of motivation is strengthened by the abandonment among the learned of a strong sense of ingrained nature and of what is natural to the tendencies of specific beings. It is this that led to the restriction of finality to purpose.

Let me repeat the paradox: the very restriction of method—to motor forces and external relations of part to part—excludes the rich and holistic totality of being that transcends the method; nevertheless, it permits its practitioners to disclose truths about the human person that are not available in any other way.[6] The reason for this is not far to seek: We humans are intellectual and, even more, are spiritual creatures, and so we yearn for the infinite, but we live in the finite. Nor do I think my perception mistaken that many dedicated therapists and theorists acknowledge a reality and meaning that lies

---

6. Bowlby's analysis provides impressive information, for understanding and for therapy, regarding the means by which certain psychological states and consequent behaviors can be diagnosed and treated; but it loses sight of the integral human factor in the action. In a sense there is, in his account, no agent, only a series of motor systems, so that not only final causality is lost; so too is the very root of effective causality, viz., the integral human person. In a word, despite his move away from Freud's physicalism to control theory, action itself gives way to process, after the manner of the physical sciences, in which motion rather than agency is the core medium and measure of interpretation and explanation.

Guidance and Finality

I should like to speak of finality's presence "advising," rather than "determining," but that would hold only in self-conscious and deliberate action. "Guidance" also is too close to our physical language, so that perhaps an analogy might serve: to suggest the inflowing of a final cause in the manner of a musical score, not understood as a printed copy, but as a directive "map" operative in the very performance of the musicians. No effective music is performed by them unless it is effectively embedded in the performance of conductor and orchestra, but in such a performance (in already created musical compositions) the music is "guided" by such a score, printed or mental. Perhaps a simpler case might be made by comparing the intrinsic presence of a final cause within a dynamic agent after the manner of a color resident in a wall orienting the eye in a determinate manner yet inseparable from the wall, and so not an entity or force in its own right. The failure of this reference, as of all such analogies, is that the color in the paint can be understood as a separable physical entity, and even as light waves in the atmosphere.

beyond the grasp of their method. Though this is a cause for wonder, it is not a cause for surprise, since, in philosophy as well, reality outstrips any exhaustive grasp on our part. No less a figure than Jaak Panksepp acknowledges: "I do not believe that distinct neurochemical systems will ever be found for such higher feelings."[7]

Nevertheless, the disclosure effected by psychic research into the unconscious and pre-conscious inner reaches of the human person is one of the several wonders of the world![8] In my opinion, far from re-

---

7. *Affective Neuroscience: The Foundations of Human and Animal Emotions* (Oxford: Oxford University Press, 1998), p. 301. He remarks (p. 226): "The biological constraints that all mammals share contain no prescription for what human sexual behavior should be. As always, in the subcortical reaches of the brain, the evidence can only tell us what *is*, it does not inform us about what *should* or *could* be, especially when it comes to creatures as complex as humans." And further (p. 230): "This is not to say that humans cannot choose to override these mechanisms with their free will. They certainly can . . . ." And more generally still (p. 247): "Among humans, biology is not necessarily destiny, because we have the ability to make cognitive choices."

8. R. Lane and L. Nadel, eds., *Cognitive Neuroscience of Emotion* (Oxford: Oxford

ducing the human person to an impersonal system of forces, it reveals an amazing design causing a researcher to ask: Can there be a design without a designer?—leaving the question of origin unanswered and perhaps for many unanswerable, at least by the method. Indeed, Seligman rejects the notion of an originating cause and suggests a developmental principle of adaptation.

Although from a philosophical perspective the psychological account is incomplete in its findings, they are, as far as they go, impressive in their detail. For example, A. Damasio sketches three somatosensory subsystems: the autonomic ("independent of our will . . . located in the brain stem, hypothalamus, and limbic nuclei"), the proprioceptive and kinesthetic (for willed moving of body parts); and the fine-touch subsystem that "signals the alterations which specialized sensors in the skin go through").[9] He thus recognizes two types of biological change: those related to the state of the body, and those related to the state of cognition.[10] True to his biological focus, however, he finds the raison d'être of consciousness to be the survival of the individual organism.[11] Yet he is clearly uncertain about the aspect of subjectivity that seems to attend conscious awareness, an aspect that does not seem to be accounted for by the two pathways engaging the brain's activity: that of the bloodstream via "chemical molecules . . .

University Press, 2000), comment, in the preface, on "a new approach . . . harnessing the concepts and methods of cognitive neuroscience . . . that honor known anatomical and functional properties of the human brain."

9. *The Feeling of What Happens*, pp. 151–53.

10. Ibid., p. 281. He also provides a brief but relatively detailed description of the CNS (central nervous system), its structure and role (pp. 325–33).

11. "I would say that consciousness . . . constrains the world of imagination to be first and foremost about the individual, about an individual organism, about the self in the broad sense of the term. I would say that the effectiveness of consciousness comes from its unabashed connection to the non-conscious proto-self. This is the connection that guarantees that proper attention is paid to the matter of individual life by creating a *concern*. Perhaps the secret behind the efficacy of consciousness is selfness. Consciousness is valuable because it centers knowledge on the life of an individual organism" (ibid., p. 304).

Intelligence and Design or Meaning and Purpose?

The question of whether there is design without a designer has been raised in contemporary psychological approaches to human happiness, meaning, and purpose. Martin E. P. Seligman, in his book *Authentic Happiness* (New York: Free Press, 2002), raises serious difficulties with such a possibility. In the chapter "Meaning and Purpose" he wrestles with the issue: "The occasion is a conclave of ten scientists, philosophers, and theologians [sponsored by the Templeton Foundation] gathered to discuss whether evolution has a purpose and a direction. A few years ago, this question would have struck me as a nonstarter, ... but [Bob Wright's *NonZero*] is so startlingly original and tightly rooted in science that it has become the springboard to my thinking about how to find meaning and purpose" (p. 250). He then reviews the difficulties in the way of accepting a designer: When his interlocutor comments, "I thought you were a nonbeliever," Seligman replies, "I am. At least I was. I've never been able to choke down the idea of a supernatural God who stands outside of time, a God who designs and creates the universe. As much as I wanted to, I [have] never been able to believe there was any meaning in life beyond the meaning we choose to adopt for ourselves. But now I'm beginning to think I was wrong, or partly wrong.... I tread much more cautiously now. I don't read the theology literature.... I have wavered between the comfortable certainty of atheism and the gnawing doubts of agnosticism my entire life, but reading Bob's manuscript has changed this. I feel ... the intimations of something vastly larger than I am or than human beings are. I have intimations of a God that those of us who are long on evidence and short on revelation (and long on hope, but short on faith) can believe in" (pp. 257–58). But serious doubts arise concerning evil, freedom, the origin of a first Principle: Ready to concede a God Who might be omnipotent, omniscient, and good, he cannot accept such a God as Creator. "If God is the designer, and also good, omniscient, and omnipotent, how come the world is so full of innocent children dying, of terrorism, and of sadism? The Creator property also contradicts human free will. How can God have created a species endowed with free will, if God is also omnipotent and omniscient? And who created the Creator anyway?" (p. 259). He continues: "The problem of reconciling human free will with the four properties of God is a very tough nut. Calvin and Luther gave up human will to save God's omnipotence. In contrast to these founding Protestants, 'process' theology is a modern development that holds that God started things in motion with an eternal thrust toward increasing complexity—so far, so good. But mounting complexity entails free will and self-consciousness, and so human free will is a strong limitation on God's power. The God of process theology gives up omnipotence and omniscience to allow human beings to enjoy free will. To circumvent 'who created the Creator,' process theology gives up creation itself by claiming that the process of becoming more complex just goes on forever; there was no beginning and will be no end. So the process-theology God allows free will, but at the expense of omnipotence, omniscience, and creation. Process theology fails because it leaves God stripped of all of the traditional properties—too much of a lesser god, in my opinion" (p. 259). And with that he proposes his own solution: The difficulty lies with the notion of a Creator, a "supernatural, an intelligent and designing being who exists before time and who is not subject to natural laws.... 'Good riddance.' This leaves us with the idea of a God who had nothing whatever to do with creation, but who is omnipotent, omniscient, and righteous.... Does this God exist?" To which he replies: Not now, because of the foregoing difficulties; but to satisfy the overriding positive tendency towards evolutionary win-win solutions, we can look "toward a God who is not supernatural, a God who ultimately acquires omnipotence, omniscience, and goodness through the natural progress of win-win. Perhaps, just perhaps, God comes at the end" (p. 260). It is perhaps not surprising that an implicit faith in finality presides over the process, as a way of rescuing an ultimate intelligibility in reality.

and neuron pathways . . . electrochemical signals . . . which in turn release chemicals . . . into the bloodstream."[12]

Damasio is astonished at the unity that results from these subsystems, and he concedes that the microanalysis that he employs is in the service of an integrated entity: you or me! Moreover, he does acknowledge "the architectural design for the varied structures of our organisms. . . . There is a *Bauplan* for life and our bodies are a *Bauhaus*. . . . What remains [throughout the constant replacement of body parts] . . . is the construction plan for our organism structure. . . . Call it the spirit of the form and the spirit of the function."[13] Here again we meet the puzzle of a design without a designer, since evolutionary adaptation may describe evolving organization but not its primordial directive finality.

12. Ibid., p. 67; also, pp. 133–36: The stable regulatory systems, beginning with the cytoplasm of the cells, the organelles, the mitochondria and microtubules—all of this achieves the needed homeostasis within the cell and ultimately achieves the complexity of the individual as a system.

13. Ibid., p. 144. The meaning of "spirit" is left vague, and indeed he uses metaphorical language to express his intuitions: such as, the mind "mapping" different objects (p. 21), and of "the movie-in-the-brain," though he recognizes the problem of accounting for the self, "the owner and observer for that movie . . . generating the *appearance of an owner and observer* within the movie" (p. 11)—to which one may well offer the rejoinder: Do we see movies or real things?

Bowlby provides practical reasons of survival for the role of automatic reactions, observing that it may take too long for consciousness to calculate danger and react to it.[14] This focus on survival leads him to attribute a considerable importance to the role of the nonconscious and pre-conscious, even to asserting that "sensory inflow can be processed outside a person's awareness to a state sufficient for much of its meaning to be determined."[15]

In keeping with the predominant value of survival, the bioneuroscientific approach discloses the subjective adaptations of the organism to its needs in relation to its environment: "in a variety of primal situations: (1) the search for food, water, and warmth; (2) the search for sex and companionship; (3) the need to care for offspring; (4) the urge to be reunited with companions after separation; (5) the urge to avoid pain and destruction; (6) the urge to express oneself vigorously with decisive actions . . . ; (7) the urge to exhibit vigorous social interactions, and perhaps several others."[16]

Two features of particular significance for philosophy emerge from this psychological research into the physical basis of emotions and interaction. The first is that—contrary to extreme philosophical rationalisms and idealisms—human intellectuality relies in indispensable ways upon the pre-determined *automatic* processes of the human composite. These processes act in accord with human nature in order to guide and effectuate outcomes absolutely vital to the survival and continuing operation of the person; examples of these elemental processes are breathing, instinctual bonding, avoidance behavior, and the like.

14. John Bowlby, *Separation, Anxiety and Anger,* Vol. II of *Attachment and Loss* (New York: Basic Books/Perseus Group, 1973, 1999), p. 152. See also *Loss, Sadness and Depression,* Vol. III of *Attachment* (New York: Basic Books/Perseus Group, 1980), p. 45: "All such processing is influenced by central control and is done at extraordinary speeds; and all but the most complex is done outside awareness." He adds the incisive observation that, whereas in the healthy psyche exclusion is both normal and adaptive, in psychopathology what is of specific interest is "what is being excluded, by what means it is excluded, and perhaps above all why it should be excluded."

15. Bowlby, *Loss, Sadness, and Depression,* p. 47.

16. Panksepp, *Affective Neuroscience,* p. 50.

The second significant feature is the largely unconscious selective suppression of data that would overburden the sensory receptors[17]—a selectivity whose principles are determined in part by survival needs, in part by what we might call temperament and interest, and in part by what we might refer to as personal character. Whereas this unconscious and pre-conscious set of processes reduces the claim to any pure rationality on the part of humans, it enhances the superbly ordered make-up that is consonant with the rational character of the human being.[18] Once again, we see the texture of being playing its role in the constitution of the human person, contributing unity, relationality, intelligibility, and value (unum, aliquid, verum, and bonum) operative in the human composite.[19]

It is not a large step from the physiological foundations of the brain and bloodstream to the grounding of emotions in the neurological structure of the human composite. "One of the goals of the field of affective neuroscience is to dissect emotion into its elementary mental operations and its corresponding neural substrates, a strategy comparable to that which is pursued for cognition within the field of

17. Panksepp (ibid., p. 165): "Evolution has automated and eliminated choice in the most important aspects of homeostasis," e.g., as in breathing, which remains at a totally "subconscious level." But also: "Feeding controls are subservient to the body's energy-regulating processes" (p. 172). And: "Stimuli that promote a return to homeostasis are routinely experienced as pleasurable, while those that would impair homeostasis are unpleasant or even distressing. . . . Useful stimuli are those that inform the brain of their potential to restore the body towards homeostatic equilibrium" (p. 182).

18. "These [neural] systems help create a substantial portion of what is traditionally considered universal 'human nature'" (ibid., p. 15).

19. Panksepp (ibid., p. 301) is not incorrect in his critique of pure mentalism, based—as his critique is—upon a justifiable rejection of Cartesian dualism, though the last sentence below needs qualification: "Although the higher cerebral functions have led to the great achievements of humankind . . . they have also generated the illusory half-truth that humans are rational creatures above all else. Despite the appeal of the rational fallacy, our higher brain areas are not immune to the subcortical influences we share with other creatures. . . . In [the special circumstances of] emotional turmoil, the upward influences of subcortical emotional circuits on the higher reaches of the brain are stronger than the top-down controls."

cognitive neuroscience."[20] Panksepp (p. 20) readily accepts the limitations of the neuroscientific approach: "Here we will proceed with the data-based premise that the ultimate sources of human feelings are biological. . . . The present view will be a reductionistic one where we shall seek the sources of emotionality within the evolutionarily shared neurodynamics of the older part of the mammalian brain."

At the same time he acknowledges Heinz Pagels's suggestion "that we need to seriously consider the fundamental correctness of the traditional materialist worldview, which has long been distasteful to humanistically oriented scholars."[21] And he adds (p. 26) his own opinion that "the innate emotional systems interact with higher brain systems so extensively that in the normal animal there is probably no emotional state that is free of cognitive ramifications. It is more likely that in humans there may be some thoughts that are free of [emotional] affect." Surely this is an opening to the subjectivity and objectivity of human cognition! This is a remarkable sensitivity that never quite escapes the method.

Before we take such a large step, however, we must look at a very remarkable dimension, that of sensory perception, which we share with the higher animals. I have already remarked upon its specifically non-invasive character, which places it in a dimension not entirely accounted for by the mutational power of physical forces; and yet it

20. Lane and Nadel, eds., *Cognitive Neuroscience of Emotion*, p. 5. Panksepp (*Affective Neuroscience*, pp. 4–6) proposes to "create a general foundation for all of psychology . . . by focusing on the shared emotional and motivational processes of the mammalian brain." But he complains that in spite of ethology, behaviorism, the cognitive sciences, sociobiology and evolutionary psychology, what is lacking in the various approaches is "an adequate neuroconceptual foundation of the sources of emotionality." And he proposes "to bring neurological issues to bear on the grand old questions concerning the nature of the human mind." At the same time, he acknowledges (p. 20) that the approach will be reductionist (see above in the text).

21. *The Dreams of Reason: The Computer and the Rise of the Sciences of Complexity* (New York: Simon and Schuster, 1988), pp. 11–12; cited by Panksepp, *Affective Neuroscience*, at p. 21.

is bound very closely to them. For, as already said, an animal sees its prey and its danger; insofar as it simply sees it, the seeing does not change the outside world, although its own subjective state alters into the desire or fear upon which it acts. Yet it is important to remark that the seeing as such and in itself does not change the thing seen, though it participates in the light waves required by the act of seeing, as well as in the physical forces that actuate sound and smell. Moreover, as already said, the seeing is bound to the particular time-space situation in which it occurs, so that there is a very intimate and inseparable binding of sense and physical reality at play in the perception, both internal and external. It is not just light waves that affect the eye but these particular light waves and their energy that activate the visual receptors, the neural pathways, and the activity of the brain.

It is just here, however, that we need to be very precise, and distinguish the physical forces that are inseparable from the processes of seeing and the sensory translation of these forces into a non-force medium, into that which I have referred to, several times, as non-invasive. And this translation is done by an agent—animal or human—with the faculty or power to make such a translation into a radically non-physical medium. We are not used to thinking in this way, preferring to reduce the eye to the workings of a camera; but a camera takes pictures, whereas we and other animals *see* things. In photography we have the unity of an operating system, whereas in a perceiving animal we have, not a camera, but an agent, a unitary being capable of initiating activity. This is an entity that escapes, even as it transcends, the limitations of a mechanistic method, which can describe the agent only in the reductionistic terms of process among externally related parts.[22]

The bonding of physical forces and the sensory powers is even more pronounced in touch. The relationship is brought out in consummate detail by the preparatory and more general work of Moberg and others on the role of the bonding reagent and hormone oxyto-

22. See fnn. 6, 13, and 20.

cin.[23] It is described as "the over-all system that produces calm and connection."[24] We have already referred in the last two footnotes to the physiology of internal factors within the central nervous system and only mention the effect upon the neural pathways of the somatic nervous system in regard to muscle control, reflex reactivity, and even voluntary movement, as well as to the autonomic nervous system that controls heart-beat, circulation, digestion and breathing.[25] It is quite amazing to realize the physiological contribution to psychological states in and through this innate substance, affecting both the subjective states or moods and the outreach to external stimuli and objects, including improving the opportunities for learning through the enhancing of calm and connection, as the physical-chemical condition for such learning.[26] In the language of traditional philosophy, the

23. See K. U. Moberg, *The Oxytocin Factor*, translated from the Swedish by Roberta Francis (Cambridge, Mass.: Da Capo Press/Perseus Group, 2003).

24. Ibid., p. 9. It is further described as contributing to a sense of "receptivity, closeness, openness to relationship, and the giving of nurturing."

25. Ibid., pp. 35–36. Indeed, the central nervous system is affected by this factor: the spinal cord, which regulates pain and other reflexes; the lower brain, which regulates fight/flight and reproductive reactions; and the cerebral cortex, which plays a role in thought, memory, and planning (p. 33). "The coordination that occurs with oxytocin-producing cells is unique in physiology . . . coordination, whether of cells, effects, or individuals, is a marker for oxytocin and something that distinguishes it from many other substances in the bodies of humans and other mammals . . . this intricate branching out of nerve fibres . . . makes it possible for the body to coordinate many different physiological functions and activities, using both oxytocin and vasopressin as messengers" (p. 56).

26. Ibid., p. 70. Even more strikingly, in a section on sex and health, the author remarks about monogamy that "having sex with a stranger (in prostitution, for example) contains a certain amount of danger, something that the body registers by initiating a form of the fight or flight reaction instead of the calm and connection system. . . . It is therefore possible that monogamy and the cultural taboo against infidelity have, at least in part, a biologically adaptive basis" (p. 120). In a more general observation, the author remarks upon the proper use and the potential abuse of the substance: "When we exercise, make love, meditate, or spend time with people we like, when we are having fun and enjoying life, this substance is working in our bodies. There are also less healthy ways to release oxytocin. Alcohol, mood-altering drugs, and fatty foods certainly give us higher oxytocin levels; but sooner or later, most of us have negative consequences from these routes to calm. We need to make informed choices" (p. 176).

Touch and Words

There is some discussion among psychotherapists, inasmuch as touch poses a delicate problem of professional ethics, since touching between adults is so easily misconstrued, especially in the relation between therapist and patient. In Appendix II, "Body Counter-transference: More Questions than Answers," in *Touch* (p. 60), Sarah Benamer and Kate White remark: "An initial question raised and explored in some groups was about whether the role of the therapist is to give the client experience of a relationship that they have needed and have not had. If so, particularly since in our culture many people are touch deprived, and since loving touch is a primary biological and psychological need, does our role as therapist include the provision of loving physical touch, when the client needs it as part of the whole human experience that we offer? Is it the fear of litigation or the fear of our own bodies that stops us from touching?" On the other hand (ibid.), "another concern . . . was the potential loss of a reflective space when a therapist actually touches his or her client." And yet, as Margot Sutherland observes in Appendix I of *Touch*, "The Neurobiology of Attachment, Touch and the Body in Early Development" (p. 58): "there are times when words are not enough."

above strikingly confirms and reinforces the insight into the close entitative and substantial unity of form and matter that make up the individual human being. Moreover, it provides an example of the consonance between the human fabric and the texture of being, with its transcendental properties of order and the good.

The research on the bonding qualities of oxytocin provides an entry into both attachment bonds and the intimate, direct, and concrete sense of touch.[27] As Bowlby points out, touch is of especial importance during the early years of infancy in the mother-child relation, but he insists that it is also vital "in the life of man from the cradle to the grave," and that touch consists in "seeking and maintaining proximity to another individual."[28] Indeed, touch is so important for in-

---

27. See the John Bowlby Memorial Conference Monograph 2003, *Touch: Attachment and the Body*, ed. Kate White (London: Karnac Books/Perseus Group, 2004), as well as Bowlby's volumes on attachment cited previously.

28. Bowlby, *Attachment*, p. 208.

timacy with others and for contact with reality that we use it analogously (if not metaphorically) in such expressions as "'being touched' through words, body language, eye contact, and the sound, musicality, physicality, and rhythm of the voice."[29] It is paradoxical that this most bodily of senses is the one that delivers the most immediate appreciation of the reality of existing persons and things. And in the most concrete of ways it affirms the relatedness that is inseparable from our very mode of being and our participation in the transcendental property of relationality *(aliquid),*[30] which is expressed colloquially in the words "Let's keep in touch."

As I recapitulate these brief remarks on the role of the emotions and the sensory powers within the unity of form and matter that constitutes the human composite, it is remarkable how many are the ways in which both the emotions and the senses mediate between our physical nature (and the world we immediately encounter), on the one hand, and the distinctively human mode of our personal being, on the other. For the emotions and the senses are at once both reactive (upon ourselves) through moods and emotions, and informative (about the world) through emotions and sense perceptions. They provide the basic data on which intellectual disclosure relies even as it transcends the limitations of our embodied situation. And it is to this intellectual modality within us that I now turn.

Panksepp warns us not to take our pretensions to cognitive achievement too seriously, since (he insists) "the brain mechanisms for language were designed for social interactions not for the conduct of science." This does not deter him, however, from proceeding to construct "a credible scientific view."[31] At any rate, the scientific en-

---

29. *Touch,* Appendix II, p. 61.

30. Colwyn Trevarthen's article "Intimate Contact from Birth: How We Know One Another by Touch, Voice, and Expression in Movement," in *Touch* (p. 2) develops a "theory of companionship," and (at p. 7) a theory of "innate intersubjectivity."

31. *Affective Neuroscience* (p. 302): "Our exquisite ability to transcribe into verbal symbols may be a lens that distorts reality as readily as it reveals it; evolutionarily,

terprise is founded upon the capacity of the human mind to engage reality and to arrive at a reliable understanding of much of it, as long as the knower exercises a critical capability as well. And indeed, the same author observes that, whereas "all mammals appear to experience pain, anger, fear, and many other raw feelings, . . . they do not seem able to cognitively reflect upon such feelings as we do."[32]

It is remarkable that, even with infants, eye contact carries with it more than light waves, infused (as it is) with verbal meaning.[33] Indeed, even more remarkable still is our capacity to understand one another—or, as Bowlby puts it, "to see things through another's eyes." He remarks that this "is an ability that develops only slowly," an ability that is increased through the communicative "gift of language."[34] Indeed, one observer insists that "memory, language, and intelligence

the brain mechanisms for language were designed for social interactions, not for the conduct of science." Yet, a few pages later he restores some of what he has taken away: "Affective neuroscience seeks to provide conceptual bridges. . . . Introspective access to primitive feelings may also provide a credible scientific view, albeit indirect" (p. 304).

32. Ibid., p. 300.

33. Bowlby, *Attachment* (vol. I, pp. 318–19) agrees with Mary Ainsworth ("The Development of Infant-Mother Interaction among the Ganda," in *Determinants of Infant Behavior*, vol. 2, ed. B. M. Foss [New York: Wiley, 1963], and *Infancy in Uganda: Infant Care and the Growth of Attachment* [Baltimore: Johns Hopkins University Press, 1967]) that the most important formative factor in development is not routine care, but social interaction; and he remarks that "from quite early weeks, an infant's eyes and ears are active in mediating social interchange, and they call in question the special role hitherto attributed to tactile and kinaesthetic stimulation . . . eye-to-eye contact also seems to play a very special part in developing a bond between infant and mother." I would only add that touch seems to play a more immediate, concrete, and existential role in attachment, whereas eye and ear play more incipient cognitive roles. Moreover, it is quite astounding that the least immediately physical of the senses—vision—should play such a revelatory role in the disclosure of interior feelings and states of consciousness.

34. Ibid., pp. 352–54. As to the pace of development, Bowlby (vol. III, *Loss, Sadness, and Depression*, pp. 426–29) observes that the child gradually develops a recognition of persons, then of things "existing independently of themselves," and then proceeds to language as the symbolic representation of the external world "by purely cognitive means."

make the difference, not emotion.... In short, consciousness is a grand permit into civilization."[35]

This somewhat sceptical author of the study of the emotions, already referred to, concedes that "obviously, in humans the role of cognitive factors, for better and worse, can often override emotional concerns."[36] Others observe that, whereas Freud laid primary emphasis on the priority of emotion over thought, still others have reversed that priority.[37] Thus, Lane and Nadel suggest a reconciliation that addresses the relation of reason and emotion in positive terms: "In contrast to the position that reason and emotion oppose one another, there is increasing recognition that in the realm of stable personal attributes and characteristics, increasing cognitive sophistication and increasing emotional sophistication can be consistent with one another."[38] The affirmation of a harmonious relation between emo-

35. A. Damasio, *The Feeling of What Happens.* After distinguishing core consciousness, the proto-self, and extended consciousness, he remarks: "Extended consciousness allows human organisms to reach the very peak of their mental abilities. Consider some of these: the ability to create helpful artifacts; the ability to consider the mind of the other; the ability to sense the minds of the collective; the ability to suffer with pain as opposed to just feel pain and react to it; the ability to sense the possibility of death in the self and in the other; the ability to value life; the ability to construct a sense of good and of evil distinct from pleasure and pain; the ability to take into account the interests of the other and of the collective; the ability to sense beauty as opposed to just feeling pleasure; the ability to sense a discord of feeling and later a discord of abstract ideas, which is the source of the sense of truth." In this summary the author has touched upon the transcendental properties of being, in particular, the relational, the good, the true and the beautiful.

36. Panksepp, *Affective Neuroscience,* pp. 266–67.

37. Seligman, *Authentic Happiness,* p. 65: "These two views [emotivism and cognitivism] have never been reconciled. The imperialistic Freudian view claims that emotion always drives thought, while the imperialistic cognitive view claims that thought always drives emotion. The evidence, however, is that each drives the other *at times* [italics mine]. So the question for twenty-first century psychology is this: under what conditions does emotion drive thinking, and under what conditions does thinking drive emotion?" And he replies: "I am not going to attempt a global resolution here, only a local one." Whereupon he offers tactical (cognitive) suggestions for the amelioration of negative emotions.

38. Lane and Nadel, eds. *Cognitive Neuroscience of Emotion,* p. 346. They refer in

tion and cognition invites a further look at the nature of cognition. In Chapter 3, I argued the case for the non-invasive and non-physical character of the knowing relation; in view of the considerable emphasis now laid upon the physiological basis of cognition and its association with emotion in the psychological literature, let me revisit this topic with what may seem an overly simple example and at the cost of seeming repetition.

Consider a carpenter and his hammer at a building site. If he is to build, he must enter the field of forces; if, during a rest break, he is to merely observe, he enters the non-invasive field of sensory perception that is tied to those forces he and others have been employing; if he is to plan or design further work, he takes these physical forces and sensory perceptions with him up to a new dimension that transcends them. For he enters a dimension where no nail is driven into physical wood, a dimension that is capable of disclosing what things are in their being (it is the dimension where the scientific mind also lives in its own methodical way).

But here precision and measure take on a new mode and meaning, where a line is neither the visual or felt line, nor its physical embodiment, but solely its mathematical properties; in short, it is an idealized line. Such a line is no longer living in its prior bodily habitat, nor merely in its visible manifestation; and yet it exists in relation to the carpenter-designer-builder, present to him in a distinct way which, far from betraying the nature of the line, actually for the first time more fully reveals its essential character!

We see, then, that the cognitive relation to the line is not just an abstract withdrawal from reality, as we tend to think, but the disclosure of the true nature of the line. Moreover, this intellectual mode of existence is not unreal. For the thought with the power to disclose such reality must itself be real, not in the way physical things are real, yet in a way that transcends both the physical and sensory conditions

---

this passage to S. Sommers, "Emotionality reconsidered: the role of cognition in emotional responsiveness," *Journal of Personality and Social Psychology* 41 (1981): 553–61.

of existence as it participates in the modality of spiritual existence in disclosing the line.

It is a paradox that the withdrawal to a non-physical modality is the pass-key to the disclosure of physical reality. As we have already said, our coming to know something about a thing in the world does nothing to that thing; nothing happens to it through our coming to know about it. Further, what happens to us is not accounted for simply by a physical mutation which would enclose the thing in us rather than disclose it in itself. For knowing the thing is not the same as digesting it—although mutations are attendant and enabling instrumentalities required by our composite being for this transcendent relation to things (i.e., to knowing). The physical mutations may describe the image-processing that attends the total experience of human knowing—for it is not a pure spirit who knows—and we draw our energy from our composite substantial being that includes within it the modality that transcends the physical. But, contrary to the materialist and positivist, we are not a film production company simply making images within our head. Knowing activity is explosive in that it breaks us loose from the material forces we embody in order to establish non-invasive relations with the things we come to know.

If what amounts to the non-materialistic, non-physical distinguishing principle within the knowing person is true—and if the knower lives in that dimension—there remains a last consequence of such a mode of existence, which traditionally has been called "spirit." For if such knowing can disclose the very nature of things (to whatever limited degree), if such knowing does bring us into relation with things as they really are in their natures, by a non-physical and non-invasive presencing, this relation opens up a universal horizon of intelligibility and meaning which is the prior condition for the expression of ideas in and through language and the condition for the pursuit of science.

Now such an initial outreach is abstract in the sense that it is relatively empty of the content that is borne by individual instantiations of being. For we have reached the level of universal intelligibility, in

Freedom and Aggression

It is significant that Panksepp, while stressing the material basis for human cognition and emotions, finds negative reasons for admitting the role of freedom by citing the disastrous misuse of it by man: "At the outset I wish to make one disclaimer: the most broadly destructive kinds of human aggression—wars between nations and competing cultural groups, as well as many violent crimes—do not arise directly from brain circuits of the type discussed here" (*Affective Neuroscience,* p. 187). In this disclaimer he relieves human nature *as such* of willed violence and leaves room for the misdirection of freedom and inhumanity, presumably by individuals and groups. He further concedes that "the higher cerebral abilities must be taken into account in any comprehensive explanation of angry behavior, and it is incorrect to believe that a study of animals will fully explain why humans exhibit and inhibit aggression" (p. 190). The significance of the turn to positive psychology is that, without its head in the sand, it investigates the challenge of human freedom in a more positive vein.

which we formulate the definitions of the various species, such as man, and of the genera, such as animal, but also of the elements, such as oxygen, and the compounds, which chemistry labors to define. The unlimited world of universal intelligibilities opens up to us and with it the required condition, not only for knowledge, but also for the exercise of freedom.

This explosive burst into the open horizon of universal meaning is the condition for our freedom, with its dangers as well as its promise. Insofar as that horizon opens up to us, so do the possibilities of choice among the various real and apparent goods. The texture of being may well offer us the true and the good, but the mixture of reality also offers us dark shadows and thieves that masquerade in the garb of those very transcendental properties. Indeed, the finite order in which we live presents the transcendental values in limited versions, and in conditions in which they may be more apparent than real or even come into seeming conflict with one another. Moreover, in their finite embodiment, they are subject to deprivation, through injury or corruption, as in the cataclysms of nature which might serve nature well but humanity poorly. Even more privative is the special deviance that arises out of the misuse of our liberty and distracts us from the inclinations pre-given in our nature, inclinations that are no longer processes but directive actions taken up into agency.

It is here that Martin Seligman, while taking account of the neurological factors of human action, yet acknowledges the determining role played by self-conscious and voluntary decision making that is open to the development of what he terms our "signature strengths"[39] and that, in large measure, correspond to what Aristotle had termed the "virtues."[40] For character is built upon personality, not just by subjective determination but by drawing power from the contextual ex-

39. *Authentic Happiness*, p. 23: Signature strengths "are deeply characteristic of you." He comments on the ubiquity of six virtues: wisdom and knowledge, courage, love and humanity, justice, temperance, spirituality and transcendence (p. 133); and he lists twenty-four strengths! (pp. 134–61). See the foundational study of these, organized around the six virtues, in: *Character Strengths and Virtues: A Handbook and Classification*, authored by Christopher Peterson and Martin Seligman, with the collaboration of forty contributors (Oxford: American Psychological Association, 2004). See also the extraordinarily rich set of essays in *A Psychology of Human Strengths: Fundamental Questions and Future Directions for a Positive Psychology*, ed. Lisa Aspinwalt and Ursula Staudinger (Washington, D.C.: American Psychological Association, 2003), a mélange of some forty-four authors, including contributions by distinguished psychologists from the United States, Europe, and Canada.

40. With the support of the Mayerson Foundation, Seligman and Peterson broadened a "positive youth development" project in association with positive psychology that built upon "people's strengths and aspirations" into "the classification and measurement strategies . . . [that] . . . can be applied much more broadly" (*Character Strengths and Virtues*, Preface, p. v). In their concluding chapter, "Assessment and Applications" (pp. 625–44), they provide a critical assessment of the state of research at this time. What is of especial importance is the variety of methods relied on, as well as the respect shown for the differences of accessibility among the various virtues and strengths: "Almost all the strengths in our classification have been the subject of empirical research using various strategies of assessment" (p. 641). The positive character of the investigation is reflected in such questions as: "What are the natural homes for human excellence?" (p. 639). And the conclusion points towards further work in integrating the findings of the various strengths with one another. This is a striking convergence of mutual concern and reinforcement between psychology and philosophy.

istentials that are the transcendental properties resident in the texture of being. Human character is developed subjectively through transforming a "career into a calling" (p. 172), by living such positive relations as trust, hope, and courage "in the service of a greater good," and objectively by participation in the values inherent in the texture of being. For what philosophers call 'natural law' is not a negative and external set of prohibitive rules, but the invitation to participate freely, positively, and intimately in the existential power of the transcendental properties of being, of unity, relationality, the true, and the good, and—if one is sensitive aesthetically and artistically—of beauty. It is just this that is meant by the elusive—and in modern thought, controversial—concept of final causality, which is embedded in our human nature and consonant with the values inherent in the texture of being.[41] Of crucial importance, therefore, is the distinction Seligman makes between pleasures and gratifications—the latter playing a role in the development of character.[42]

It is striking that the turn to positive psychology is entirely consonant with the transcendental properties in the texture of being. Thus, Bowlby,[43] remarking on the role of attachment figures and early fam-

41. See, in lieu of an acknowledgment of final causality, the discussion of "flow" as well as "intrinsic motivation" in Alan Carr, *Positive Psychology* (London: Routledge, 2004), pp. 46–47; see also Seligman (*Authentic Happiness*, pp. 166, 172) on calling. Concerning the calling, we might ask: From where does the call come, if not from both within (embedded in human nature) and without (in the texture of being)?

42. See *Authentic Happiness*, p. 102; and remarks on Aristotle's *eudaimonia* (p. 112) as well as Seligman's prescription for the good life as consisting in using one's "signature strengths" (p. 121). See also Carr, *Positive Psychology* (p. 39), who distinguishes hedonic and eudaimonic states, the latter "achieving one's potential" (pp. 51–53); following Seligman, Carr points to "character strengths" as "routes for achieving virtues," as well as "enabling conditions" (such as role models and safe environment) and "personality traits" (such as love of learning, zest, perseverance, teamwork, awe, gratitude and spirituality) (pp. 51–54).

43. *Separation, Anxiety and Anger*, p. 322: "There is a strong case for believing that unthinking confidence in the unfailing accessibility and support of attachment figures is the bedrock on which stable and self-reliant personality is built"; also pp. 323, 331–42, and 344–59.

ily environment, provides evidence of what the philosopher—or at least this philosopher—understands is grounded in ontological trust in the texture of being. Nor should this trust be a deliberate disregard for the evils and privations we encounter in the mixture of reality, but it should support a determination to promote the path to maturity through the task of discovery and recovery. Seligman counsels us to seek out the "strengths and virtues that are ubiquitous, that are valued in virtually every culture," the gratifications that complete our maturity.[44] This is the humanistic and personal task to which each of us is called, the development of the virtues. For these virtues are more than moral rules for the enforcement of right and wrong. They are the transcendental "food" upon which our well-being is nourished and by which it nourishes itself. The development of character in and through the practice of the virtues recovers the values inherent in the texture of being from the mix of reality in which we encounter them.

It is just this that the philosophers mean by natural law. The psychological research on the physiological basis for that law brings out the early pre-given dynamics that provide a sort of material and formal a priori that inclines (but does not compel) a human agent to act in certain ways.[45] Thus, along with Panksepp's view, Bowlby's attachment theory, operative in neo-natal behavior, illustrates the highly programmed and pre-oriented inclinations that provide the basis for the later development of human nature, anticipating its mature form. These inclinations form the basis upon which—with deliberate knowledge, selection, choice, decision, and performance—the life of virtues is able and is meant to be enacted. Jacques Maritain, among the philosophers, has highlighted the notion of the inclinations of human nature as the genesis of natural law (in his analysis based upon the texts of St. Thomas Aquinas, which we mentioned above). Natural law is here understood as the pre-rational orientation inborn in the

44. *Authentic Happiness*, p. 102.
45. See St. Thomas Aquinas on "natural inclinations," *Summa theologiae* I-II, qq. 90ff.

human agent and his or her nature—an orientation that is intended to be taken up into an intellectual and spiritual dimension, and integrated within the cognitional and voluntary dynamism of the human person. Here both substantial form (human nature) and finality (human good) are seen as constitutive principles of the person.[46] Indeed, a traditional philosopher sees all four causes in play: the material cause providing the physiological structure, as forming the base and source of certain potentialities; the formal cause (substantial form) providing the specific unity of human nature; the final cause or telos as the soliciting and motivational aim; and the existential principle (efficient cause) as endowing the whole composite with actual being.

And so we return, after what I hope has been a rich and informative journey, to our starting point in the texture of being. The journey will not be of direct and practical assistance to the therapist in his or her remedial work; nor will it provide the needed special knowledge that research provides; but it is intended to provide a larger context and horizon, and even a very general directive compass towards the accomplishment of such a noble and therapeutic endeavor. In harmony with positive psychology, the notion of the texture of being suggests a compass to guide our ongoing endeavor of increasing our moral and ontological strengths and reducing the moral deviations and the non-moral deficiencies that arise in the mixture of reality; and to do this by appropriating the saving means within the texture of being, and by developing the inclinations of nature, which participate in that texture, into virtues: into the excellences of Aristotle, the inclinations of Thomas, and the strengths highlighted by Seligman. Human nature gives specific and limited expression to the transcendental properties of being, which the person is called upon to take up as values into the dimension of his or her freedom, where the properties play the role of virtues in the development of human character, human maturity, and

46. For Panksepp and Bowlby, see the references above; for Maritain, *The Rights of Man and Natural Law* (New York: Gordian Press, 1971); and for St. Thomas, the preceding footnote and Chapter 2.

human wisdom. The elaboration of these directive principles through our conscious freedom is the task of ethics and law.

The strengths and virtues are not restricted to moral perfections, however central and important they are in the development of our humanity, but the wider scope of virtues includes all manner of developed capacities for the appreciation of the texture of being and its values—moral and others—that are constitutive of that ontological structure in which we live and have our being. For there are vital values affecting our health and survival, technical values permitting a judicious stewardship of our environment, aesthetic values that appreciate the luminous wonder of being, intellectual values that open us out to vast spheres of meaning, and religious values that acknowledge the sublime and sacred giftedness of being.

It is, however, the moral values rooted fundamentally in the good of being, and more proximately tailored to the specificity of our human nature and personal well-being, that most directly form us in the fulfilment and maturity of our humanity; these primarily determine the value of the exercise of responsible freedom. It is just here that our freedom is called into the service of the perfection of our humanity. The other perfections receive their definitive value in and through the use we make of our liberty, for it is in that use that we exercise the initiative that is exclusively human, responsive, and responsible action that bears our personal signature.

WORKS CITED

Ainsworth, Mary D. "The Development of Infant-Mother Interaction among the Ganda." In *Determinants of Infant Behavior.* Vol. 2, edited by B. M. Foss. New York: Wiley, 1963.

————. *Infancy in Uganda: Infant Care and the Growth of Attachment.* Baltimore: Johns Hopkins University Press, 1967.

Aquinas, St. Thomas. *Basic Writings of Thomas Aquinas.* Edited by Anton C. Pegis. 2 vols. New York: Random House, 1945.

Arnold, Magda. B. *Emotion and Personality.* 2 volumes. Vol. I: *Psychological Aspects.* New York: Columbia University Press, 1961.

Aristotle. *The Basic Works of Aristotle*, edited by Richard McKeon. New York: Random House, 1941.

Aspinwalt, Lisa, and Ursula Staudinger, eds. *A Psychology of Human Strengths: Fundamental Questions and Future Directions for a Positive Psychology.* Washington, D.C.: American Psychological Association, 2003.

Benamer, Sarah, and Kate White. "Body Counter-transference: More Questions than Answers." Appendix II to *Touch, Attachment, and the Body.* The John Bowlby Memorial Conference Monograph 2003, edited by Kate White. London: Karnac Books/Perseus Group, 2004.

Bowlby, John. *Attachment and Loss.* 3 Volumes.

    Volume I: *Attachment.* New York: Basic Books/Perseus Group, 1969; 2d ed. 1982.

    Volume II: *Separation, Anxiety, and Anger.* Basic Books/Perseus Group, 1973.

Volume III: *Loss, Sadness, and Depression*. New York: Basic Books/ Perseus Group, 1980.

Carr, Alan. *Positive Psychology*. London: Routledge, 2004.

Damasio, Antonio *The Feeling of What Happens: Body, Emotion and the Making of Consciousness*. London: Vintage, 2000.

Descartes, René. *A Discourse on Method*. Oxford: Oxford University Press, 2006.

Gorer, Geoffrey. "Death, Grief and Mourning in Britain." In *The Child in His Family: The Impact of Disease and Death*, ed. E. J. Anthony and C. Koupernik, pp. 423–24. New York: J. Wiley, 1973.

La Mettrie, Julien Offray de. *Man a Machine*. Chicago: Open Court, 2007.

Lane, Richard, and Lynn Nadel, eds. *Cognitive Neuroscience of Emotion*. Oxford: Oxford University Press, 2000.

Maritain, Jacques. *The Rights of Man and Natural Law*. New York: Gordian Press, 1971.

Moberg, Kersten U. *The Oxytocin Factor*. Translated from the Swedish by Roberta Francis. Cambridge Mass.: Da Capo Press/Perseus Group, 2003.

Pagels, Heinz. *The Dreams of Reason: The Computer and the Rise of the Sciences of Complexity*. New York: Simon and Schuster, 1988.

Panksepp, Jaak. *Affective Neuroscience: The Foundations of Human and Animal Emotions*. Oxford: Oxford University Press, 1998.

Peters, F. E. *Greek Philosophical Terms*. New York: New York University Press, 1967.

Peterson, Christopher, Martin Seligman, et al. *Character Strengths and Virtues: A Handbook and Classification*. Oxford: American Psychological Association, 2004.

Plato. *Dialogues of Plato*. Translated by Benjamin Jowet. 2 vols. New York: Random House, 1937.

Ratzinger, Joseph Cardinal [subsequently Pope Benedict XVI]. *"In the Beginning . . ." A Catholic Understanding of the Story of Creation and the Fall*. Translated by Boniface Ramsey, O.P. Grand Rapids, MI: Wm. Eerdmans, 1995.

Schmitz, Kenneth. "The Geography of the Human Person" *Communio* 13 (1986): 27–48. Reprinted in *The Texture of Being*. Washington, D.C.:

The Catholic University of America Press, 2007, pp. 149–67.

Seligman, Martin. *Authentic Happiness.* New York: Free Press, 2002.

Sommers, Shula. "Emotionality Reconsidered: The Role of Cognition in Emotional Responsiveness." *Journal of Personality and Social Psychology* 41 (1981): 553–61.

Sutherland, Margot. "The Neurobiology of Attachment, Touch and the Body in Early Development." Appendix I to *Touch: Attachment, and the Body,* The John Bowlby Memorial Conference Monograph 2003, edited by Kate White, pp. 57–58. London: Karnac Books/Perseus Group, 2004.

Touch: Attachment, and the Body. The John Bowlby Memorial Conference Monograph 2003, edited by Kate White. London: Karnac Books/Perseus Group, 2004.

Trevarthen, Colwyn. "Intimate Contact from Birth: How We Know One Another by Touch, Voice, and Expression in Movement." In *Touch: Attachment, and the Body,* The John Bowlby Memorial Conference Monograph 2003, edited by Kate White, pp. 1–16. London: Karnac Books/
Perseus Group, 2004.

Wojtyła, Karol [subsequently Pope John Paul II]. *Ocena możliwości zbudowania etyki chrześcijańskiej przy założeniach systemu Maksa Schelera* [On the possibility of constructing a Christian ethic on the basis of the system of Max Scheler]. Lublin: TNKUL, 1959.

———. *Osoba i Czyn.* Polskie Towarzysto Teologiczne, 1969. Translated by A. Potocki, revised by Anna-Teresa Tymieniecka, as *The Acting Person.* Dodrecht, Holland: Reidel, 1979.

———. *Wykłady lubelskie* [Lublin lectures]. Lublin: TNKUL, 1986. (Translated into German by Juliusz Stroynowski as *Lubliner Vorlesungen.* Stuttgart: Seewald Verlag, 1981.)

INDEX OF SUBJECTS

INDEX OF NAMES

The John Henry Cardinal Newman Lectures
EDITED BY CRAIG STEVEN TITUS

1. *The Person and the Polis: Faith and Values within the Secular State* (2007)

2. *On Wings of Faith and Reason: The Christian Difference in Culture and Science* (2008)

3. *Christianity and the West: Interaction and Impact in Art and Culture* (2009)

4. *The Psychology of Character and Virtue* (2009)

Monograph Series

Fergus Kerr, *"Work on Oneself": Wittgenstein's Philosophical Psychology* (2008)

Person and Psyche was designed and typeset in Minion by Kachergis Book Design of Pittsboro, North Carolina. It was printed on 55-pound Colonial White and bound by Lightning Source of La Vergne, Tennessee.

Breinigsville, PA USA
05 October 2009
225257BV00001B/1/P